# TABLE OF CONTENTS

2 0 0 7   N a t i o n a l   M o n e y   L a u n d e r i n g   S t r a t e g y

# FOREWORD

The National Money Laundering Strategy for 2007 breaks new ground in two important respects: it responds directly to the unprecedented U.S. interagency Money Laundering Threat Assessment completed in December 2005, and it focuses exclusively on deterring money laundering, independent of our efforts to combat the financing of terror. Money laundering, in its own right, is a serious threat to our national and economic security. Integrating illicit proceeds into the financial system enables organized crime, fuels corruption, and erodes confidence in the rule of law.

The specific money laundering threats and vulnerabilities addressed by the 2007 Strategy were identified by an interagency working group in a year-long evaluation that culminated in the U.S. Money Laundering Threat Assessment. The Threat Assessment represents a significant step forward for the U.S. Government's efforts to combat money laundering and is a testament to our progress. Never before have regulators, policymakers, and law enforcement professionals come together to identify money laundering trends and methods in the United States, and to assess our effectiveness against a spectrum of money laundering threats.

Further, the 2007 Strategy builds on a solid foundation of successful initiatives and programs introduced in previous National Money Laundering Strategies. Although we have made progress, money laundering is a dynamic threat requiring a dynamic response. As globalization opens borders to travel and trade, and global payments and clearing systems evolve, new money laundering opportunities are created and exploited. Accordingly, the 2007 National Money Laundering Strategy responds to established and emerging money laundering trends and techniques both at home and abroad.


Henry M. Paulson, Jr.
*Secretary of the Treasury*

Alberto R. Gonzales
*Attorney General*

Michael Chertoff
*Secretary of Homeland Security*

# INTRODUCTION

The 2007 National Money Laundering Strategy is a direct response to the first U.S. Government-wide money laundering threat assessment released in December 2005. In addition to following this new methodology, the 2007 Strategy for the first time focuses exclusively on money laundering. Previous U.S money laundering strategies presented a combined program against both money laundering and terrorist financing. While money launderers and terrorist financiers may use the same financial channels and employ similar techniques, there are differences in their operations and in our strategies against them.

The National Money Laundering Strategy for 2007 identifies areas in which the U.S. government will work to revise, enhance, or renew efforts to enforce existing Federal laws and regulations; study areas in which new guidance may be appropriate; and work with State supervisory and law enforcement authorities to improve financial transparency in State-regulated financial sectors. There are also areas identified in which the U.S. can more effectively exploit information-sharing opportunities between law enforcement and the financial services community.

Although conceived to be the foundation for the 2007 Strategy, the U.S. Money Laundering Threat Assessment is much more than that. It not only assesses the progress the United States has made in combating money laundering and highlights areas that require further attention, but also provides lawmakers, regulators, examiners, law enforcement, and industry with a cautionary explanation of how major money laundering methods operate. For this reason, the Threat Assessment is included in its entirety as Appendix A.

Key findings of the U.S. Money Laundering Threat Assessment include:

- Banks and other depository institutions remain the primary gateway to the U.S. financial system. Once illegal proceeds get into a depository institution, they can be moved instantly by wire or disguised through commingling with legitimate funds. With the advent of Internet and remote banking, depository institutions face increased challenges identifying customers and their customers' sources of funds.

- Money Services Businesses (MSBs) offer an alternative to banks for both financial services and money laundering. This industry includes check cashers, money transmitters, foreign exchange dealers, and sellers of money orders, stored value products, and travelers' checks. Small retailers may offer informal money services as a sideline. Relatively few MSBs are registered.

- Smuggling cash out of the United States for deposit elsewhere is a well-established money laundering method and appears to be on the rise due to the barriers criminals face attempting to launder cash domestically. Bulk cash smuggling is most often associated with illegal narcotics. The illicit proceeds flow out of the U.S., often across the Southwest border, retracing the route that drugs frequently take entering the United States. Drugs and illicit proceeds cross the U.S. northern border as well.

- Often the most complex money laundering methods involve the use of international trade to disguise funds transfers. Trade-based money laundering takes many forms including the Black Market Peso Exchange, which separates the crime from the cash early in the money laundering process. Under this scheme, drug dealers are able to hand off their illicit dollars in the U.S. to professional money launderers who make clean funds available outside the United States.

- Legal entities, including corporations, limited liability companies and trusts, serve many legitimate purposes but also can be used for money laundering. Criminals who are able to hide their control of a company or trust can disguise their money laundering activity as commercial transactions. Minimal registration requirements and lax oversight can make it difficult to determine who owns and operates legal entities.

- Casinos are cash-intensive businesses that often provide financial services and money laundering opportunities. The exchange of cash for casino chips and related money transfer and account services make casinos vulnerable to money laundering. The number of gaming establishments in the U.S. is growing, driven by Native American tribes. Casinos on Indian reservations today bring in more money than Las Vegas and Atlantic City combined.

- The insurance industry has undergone a transformation, and may become increasingly attractive to money launderers. While traditional insurance policies remain an important part of the life insurance business, agents and brokers now offer a range of investment services featuring financial products that can be purchased and subsequently transferred, redeemed or sold, creating new opportunities for money laundering.

The United States has a robust and aggressive anti-money laundering (AML) program. While quantifying the effectiveness of U.S. efforts against money laundering is difficult given the nature of the crime, there are ample indications U.S. regulations and law enforcement are having an impact. As it becomes more difficult to move illicit funds using a particular money laundering method, there is a clear migration to other channels. The Financial Action Task Force recognized the effectiveness of the U.S. AML enforcement regime in its Report on the Third Mutual Evaluation of the United States adopted in June 2006. The Report's summary states:

*The U.S. Authorities are committed to identifying, disrupting, and dismantling money laundering and terrorist financing networks. They seek to combat money laundering and terrorist financing on all fronts, including by aggressively pursuing financial investigations. These efforts have produced impressive results in terms of prosecutions, convictions, seizures, asset freezing, confiscation and regulatory enforcement actions[1].*

Statistics demonstrating the Federal law enforcement and regulatory efforts against money laundering are presented in Appendix B.

The Threat Assessment and 2007 National Money Laundering Strategy are products of broad-based interagency cooperation. More than a dozen Federal agencies, bureaus, and offices participated in these projects, each with a unique mission and a unique view of the money laundering landscape. Each category of financial crime has distinct criminal and financial traits. Accordingly, each Federal law enforcement agency has a lead role in a particular category of crime and often has expertise interdicting specific money laundering threats. Participation in crafting the 2007 Strategy came from across the Departments of the Treasury, Justice, State, and Homeland Security, as well as from the Board of Governors of the Federal Reserve System, the Office of the Comptroller of the Currency, and the Federal Deposit Insurance Corporation.

Collaboration is an essential component of the U.S. strategy against money laundering. U.S. law enforcement agencies are most effective when they work together through information sharing, pooled databases, regional task forces and Suspicious Activity Report Review Teams. Examples of law enforcement collaboration are included in Appendix C, which includes a listing of databases and intelligence centers that hold bulk cash seizure and other information.

An important tool in the U.S. fight against money laundering is asset forfeiture, which strips away the profit from illegal activity. In addition to disgorging criminal proceeds and deterring crime, asset forfeiture has been used to facilitate the return of funds to victims of fraud and has resulted in millions of dollars being transferred to State, local and international law enforcement efforts through equitable sharing. A description of the strategic use of asset forfeiture is presented in Appendix D.

Due to the global nature of financial and communications networks, the United States cannot have a sustained impact against money laundering unless other countries impose similar or complementary domestic regulations and cooperate with international sanctions. The U.S. government continues to work bilaterally and multilaterally to improve global safeguards. All agencies participating in AML initiatives domestically also work closely with their international counterparts through bilateral and multilateral channels to assist in capacity-building efforts and coordination. International support for effective AML programs is vital to the national security of the United States and is one of the goals outlined in the 2007 National Money Laundering Strategy.

---

[1] Financial Action Task Force, Summary of the Third Mutual Evaluation Report on Anti-Money Laundering and Combating the Financing of Terrorism, United States of America, 23 June 2006, available at www.fatf-gafi.org/dataoecd/44/9/37101772.pdf

## Goal 1:
# CONTINUE TO SAFEGUARD THE BANKING SYSTEM

### Threats and Vulnerabilities

Banks and other depository institutions are the principal gateway to the U.S. financial system and are constantly threatened by criminals attempting to launder illicit funds. Once illegal proceeds are placed into a depository institution, the funds can be moved easily by wire transfer or disguised by intermingling them with legitimate funds. The challenges depository institutions face include criminals attempting to hide their identities and sources of income in order to open accounts and launder illicit proceeds. In addition, use of the Internet as a means for customers to open or access accounts and the steady influx of immigrants without U.S. government-issued identification are compelling banks to explore new ways to verify the identity of their customers. Internationally, the use of "correspondent," "payable through," and "nested" accounts also create opportunities for concealing a customer's true identity in the absence of adequate customer due diligence. Even when currency is smuggled out of the United States, the funds can get into the banking system abroad and come back to the U.S. via cross-border wire transfers.[2]

### Strategy

*To safeguard the banking system, the Financial Crimes Enforcement Network (FinCEN), the Federal banking regulators, and the Federal law enforcement community will continue to work closely with the banking industry to fight money laundering. FinCEN and the Federal banking regulators will develop and publish guidance alerting the banking industry to money laundering threats and the development and application of AML controls. FinCEN also will work to enhance information sharing between the law enforcement community and the banking industry, and will conduct focused outreach in coordination with law enforcement to demonstrate the value of Bank Secrecy Act data to the various sectors of the financial community. The Federal law enforcement community will make industry outreach a priority and will pursue financial crimes aggressively.*

### Action Items[3]

- FinCEN will continue to conduct outreach efforts on the new regulatory requirements implementing Section 312 of the USA PATRIOT Act. Section 312 requires certain financial institutions to conduct due diligence when establishing or maintaining correspondent accounts for foreign financial institutions or private banking accounts for non-U.S. persons and to conduct enhanced due diligence when establishing or maintaining correspondent accounts for certain types of foreign banks or private banking accounts for senior foreign political figures, their families and close associates.

- FinCEN and the Federal banking regulators will work with the Federal law enforcement agencies to shut off access to U.S. depository institutions for the Black Market Peso Exchange (BMPE) by increasing the use of advisories to alert depository institutions of relevant threats. The BMPE is considered a trade-based money laundering technique, but it often relies on access to accounts at U.S. depository institutions.[4]

- FinCEN will work to sign information-sharing agreements with States that have not yet signed a memorandum of understanding (MOU). FinCEN developed a model information-sharing agreement that it is seeking to execute with all States that regulate banks, money services businesses (MSBs), and other types of financial institutions for compliance with the Bank Secrecy Act (BSA) or similar AML requirements.

- FinCEN will place a stronger emphasis on producing more advanced analytic products and increase its ongoing efforts to analyze BSA filings to provide geographic threat assessments. These assessments help law enforcement better determine where vulnerabilities may exist in the financial systems operating within their respective geographic areas and assist the Federal and State banking regulators in targeting examinations and enforcement.

---

[2] For more information on money laundering threats to the U.S. banking system and countermeasures see Appendix A.

[3] Many of these Action Items are applicable to the broader category of "financial institutions," which includes banks and other depository institutions, as well as other financial services businesses.

[4] For more on the BMPE and trade-based money laundering see Goal 4 and Appendix A.

- FinCEN and Federal law enforcement agencies will continue information-sharing and partnering with the financial community through forums, such as the Bank Secrecy Act Advisory Group (BSAAG)[5] and its related subcommittees. FinCEN will propose to the BSAAG the creation of a new subcommittee to serve as a forum in which all stakeholders can provide input and maintain a dialogue on stored value issues as FinCEN implements its regulatory plan.

- The Treasury will work with the Federal law enforcement agencies to identify areas where Geographic Targeting Orders (GTOs) could be used to identify and attack geographically specific money laundering activity. The Treasury Department has the authority, using a GTO, to require financial institutions in a geographic area to file additional transaction reports or maintain additional records beyond those ordinarily required under the regulations implementing the BSA and other relevant requirements. GTOs have the potential to generate important information for law enforcement, facilitating better targeting of resources to combat illegal activity.

- FinCEN will facilitate improved information-sharing among and between the financial services community and law enforcement. Section 314 of the USA PATRIOT Act enables government entities to provide actionable intelligence to financial institutions, and mandates reporting by financial institutions, as well as facilitating information sharing among financial institutions themselves. FinCEN will provide more frequent alerts and advisories regarding terrorist financing and money laundering through the Section 314 information-sharing system to better educate the industry regarding risks to the U.S. financial system and enable the industry to interdict appropriately.

- FinCEN, in conjunction with other components of the Treasury, will study the application, supervision, and enforcement of AML policies and procedures on private-sector global payment networks, leveraging similar work being undertaken by a number of governmental and international organizations on a multilateral basis. The global reach of these payment networks often puts them outside the jurisdiction of any one domestic authority.

- FinCEN will work to promote consistent reporting of how BSA data is used and the value of BSA data to the relevant agencies.

- The Office of Foreign Assets Control (OFAC) will continue to foster transparency within the automated clearing house[6] community to assure that adequate information is included with cross-border funds transfers and that transactions subject to financial sanctions are appropriately interdicted.

- Federal law enforcement agencies that investigate financial crimes will expand formal outreach programs with the banking industry and identify industry liaisons.

- Federal law enforcement agencies will maintain robust Suspicious Activity Report (SAR) review programs and BSA data analysis in order to initiate and support investigations of attempts to exploit the banking system for money laundering. There are 80 SAR Review Teams operating across the United States analyzing BSA data to identify evidence of financial crimes.

---

[5] The BSAAG is an advisory group consisting of representatives of government, financial institutions, and other interested persons. The BSAAG meets semiannually for the purpose of informing private sector representatives of the utility of Bank Secrecy Act reports and to advise the Secretary of the Treasury (or his designee) of potential enhancements or modifications to existing Bank Secrecy Act requirements.

[6] The Automated Clearing House (ACH) system is a domestic electronic batch transfer interbank payment network. The ACH is used by participating depository financial institutions to clear electronic funds transfers, such as automatic payroll deposits and certain debit card transactions. The Federal Reserve and the Electronic Payments Network act as central clearing facilities through which financial institutions transmit or receive ACH entries. The ACH is governed by the private sector National Automated Clearing House Association.

# Goal 2:
# ENHANCE FINANCIAL TRANSPARENCY IN MONEY SERVICES BUSINESSES

### Threats and Vulnerabilities

C riminals unable to move illicit cash directly into the U.S. banking system may turn to money services businesses (MSBs) as an alternative. MSBs encompass a large and varied group of non-depository financial service providers offering both formal and informal value transfer services. MSBs include money transmitters, check cashers, currency exchangers, as well as issuers, sellers, and redeemers of money orders, traveler's checks, and stored value. The diversity and accessibility of the MSB sector presents challenges for regulation and oversight. While the exact number of service providers in the United States is difficult to determine, estimates suggest that fewer than 20 percent of MSBs are registered with FinCEN. It is not known what percentage of unregistered MSBs are exempt from registration, due for example to their low business volumes or agent status. Regardless, the result is that the vast majority of MSBs operate without direct Federal regulatory supervision.[7]

### Strategy

*The relevant regulatory, supervisory, and law enforcement agencies will work collaboratively to improve and expand MSB outreach initiatives and will work aggressively to identify and prosecute MSBs that facilitate money laundering. FinCEN will clarify MSB regulatory obligations, simplify the registration process, and strengthen the BSA compliance supervisory structure.*

### Action Items

- Federal law enforcement agencies will increase enforcement efforts along the Southwest border, which they have identified as a primary destination and transshipment point for suspicious funds sent through MSBs. A key finding of the 2005 National Drug Threat Assessment[8] was that drug traffickers use MSBs – particularly money transmitters, currency exchanges (*casas de cambio*), and check cashing businesses – to launder drug proceeds.

- OFAC will enter into MOUs with the States, working with the Conference of State Bank Supervisors and the Money Transmitter Regualtors Association, to share information and improve awareness of trade and economic sanctions that are often connected with money laundering schemes.

- FinCEN, in coordination with the Federal banking regulators and the industry, will issue guidance and develop regulatory definitions and requirements under the BSA for stored value products and payment systems.

- FinCEN will coordinate with the Federal law enforcement agencies and the Immigration and Customs Enforcement (ICE)-led Identity and Benefit Fraud Task Force to identify unregistered MSBs, conduct outreach and, where appropriate, to harmonize law enforcement responses. ICE's new MSB/IVTS[9] initiative has since January 2006 identified more than 400 unlicensed MSBs, resulting in the initiation of 300 criminal investigations.

- FinCEN, in coordination with the Internal Revenue Service (IRS), will enhance public sector outreach to educate MSBs about their regulatory obligations as well as making the sector aware of money laundering indicators.

- FinCEN will explore ways to obtain more information on MSBs. This will help focus supervision and enforcement resources on MSBs that present the greatest vulnerability to money laundering and other criminal activity. FinCEN also will seek to clarify the extent to which branches or agents of foreign MSBs located in the United States are subject to the BSA.

---

[7] For more information on money laundering threats involving MSBs and U.S. countermeasures see Appendix A.

[8] National Drug Threat Assessment, produced by the National Drug Intelligence Center, available at http://www.usdoj.gov/ndic/pubs11/12620/index htm.

[9] Informal Value Transfer Systems (IVTS) refers to funds transfers that take place outside of the conventional banking system through non-bank financial institutions or other business entities whose primary business activity may not be the transmission of money

- The IRS will work to sign information-sharing agreements with States that have not already signed an MOU. The IRS has a model Federal/State MOU that provides both IRS and the participating State the opportunity to leverage resources for BSA examinations, training, and outreach. FinCEN and the IRS (which has been delegated examination authority for MSBs[10]) are reviewing examiner training materials, as well as materials used for education and outreach, and are working with State regulators to launch a task force dedicated to educating and assisting MSB regulators on the conduct of BSA examinations.

- IRS-Criminal Investigation (IRS-CI) and IRS Small Business/Self Employed BSA (IRS SB/SE BSA) will continue to implement the Fraud Referral Program through which civil operating divisions of the IRS advise IRS-CI of potential criminal violations encountered during the performance of their duties. The Fraud Referral Program has been a traditional tool for criminal tax enforcement, but in FY 2005 IRS-CI, working with IRS SB/SE, expanded the program to include MSB BSA compliance.

---

[10]  IRS Small Business/Self Employed BSA has been delegated authority to examine MSBs for BSA compliance.

## Goal 3:
# STEM THE FLOW OF ILLICIT BULK CASH OUT OF THE UNITED STATES

### Threats and Vulnerabilities

C riminals facing barriers to money laundering at banks and MSBs in the United States may attempt to smuggle cash to foreign financial institutions. Often some of those funds are wired or transported back to the United States for deposit in U.S. accounts. The smuggling of bulk currency out of the United States is the largest and most significant drug-money laundering threat facing law enforcement. Deterring direct access to U.S. financial institutions by criminals does not prevent money laundering if illicit proceeds can still reach U.S. accounts through indirect means.[11]

### Strategy

*Stopping criminal proceeds from leaving the United States as illicit bulk cash and reentering the country as seemingly legitimate funds requires a borderless strategy that includes initiatives against bulk cash smuggling at home and capacity building and cooperation abroad.[12]*

### Action Items

- Treasury's Executive Office for Asset Forfeiture will provide support for both IRS-CI and ICE to establish more Federal law enforcement-led task forces and investigations targeting the smuggling of bulk cash out of the United States. The Department of Justice will provide support for Drug Enforcement Administration (DEA) participation in task forces and investigations targeting bulk cash smuggling.

- The Departments of the Treasury and Justice will continue to sponsor advanced bulk currency smuggling and post-interdiction financial investigations training for DEA, IRS-CI, ICE and Customs and Border Protection (CBP), and the United States Attorneys Offices.

- OFAC and the Federal Reserve will continue their efforts to prevent the wholesale distribution of U.S. currency, by commercial banks that receive Federal Reserve Cash Services, to rogue regimes or entities that appear on OFAC's List of Specially Designated Nationals and Blocked Persons.

- CBP, DEA, and ICE will expand bulk cash concealment detection training for State and local law enforcement. This will include training in concealment "trap" detection[13] , methods of courier debriefing, and guidance on pertinent evidence identification.

- The Organized Crime Drug Enforcement Task Force (OCDETF), through its regional strategic initiatives, will target illegal bulk cash movement along the Southwest border and on interstate highways coming from the Western and Eastern States. These bulk cash initiatives will be supported by OCDETF's Co-Located Strike Forces in Houston and Atlanta and the Gulf Coast High Intensity Drug Trafficking Area (HIDTA)[14] Blue Lightning Operations Center, which function as regional points of contact for law enforcement officers and prosecutors nationwide. These regional support centers gather intelligence and disseminate leads quickly throughout neighboring areas.

- The DHS-led Border Enforcement Security Task Force (BEST) will be expanded beyond the Southwest border, where bulk cash smuggling is

---

[11]  For more information on bulk cash smuggling and U.S. countermeasures see Appendix A.

[12]  For information on international initiatives see Goal 8.

[13]  Smugglers use many low- and high-tech methods to conceal cash and other contraband in hidden compartments or "traps" in vehicles and merchandise.

[14]  The HIDTA program enhances and coordinates drug control efforts among local, State, and Federal law enforcement agencies. The program provides agencies with equipment, technology, and additional resources to combat drug trafficking and its harmful consequences in critical regions of the United States.

targeted as an identified vulnerability at specific points of entry, to include Northern border locations as well.

- CBP, in coordination with ICE, will increase the capability for outbound inspections and will continue to invest in research and development of non-intrusive bulk currency detection technology.

- CBP, in coordination with ICE, will develop mitigation guidelines for bulk cash smuggling violations. Currently, when cash is seized in violation of the bulk cash smuggling statute, 31 U.S.C. 5332, CBP has utilized mitigation guidelines applicable to a person failing to file a Report of International Transportation of Currency or Monetary Instruments (required for amounts exceeding $10,000 entering or leaving the country). Distinct mitigation guidelines must be formulated for the smuggling of bulk currency.

- FinCEN and the Federal banking regulators will work with the Federal law enforcement agencies to help U.S. depository institutions identify illicit deposits. In April 2006, FinCEN and the Federal banking regulators issued an advisory warning that U.S. financial institutions may be misused for the repatriation of illicit U.S. currency smuggled into Mexico.

- The National Drug Intelligence Center (NDIC) will partner with the El Paso Intelligence Center[15] to produce a comprehensive Southwest border bulk cash threat assessment. This joint analysis will produce recommendations to maximize the effectiveness of law enforcement resources to combat bulk cash smuggling in the Southwest border region.

- NDIC will conduct a comprehensive analysis of bulk cash smuggling along the Northern border. The project will seek to identify the areas in this region where bulk cash smuggling is taking place, the methods used, and the groups responsible.

---

[15] See Appendix C.

## Goal 4:
# ATTACK TRADE-BASED MONEY LAUNDERING AT HOME AND ABROAD

### *Threats and Vulnerabilities*

The most complex money laundering methods are often those that use trade to transfer value into or out of the United States. Trade-based money laundering encompasses a variety of schemes. The most common in the Western Hemisphere is the Black Market Peso Exchange (BMPE) in which Colombian drug traffickers swap illicit dollars in the United States for clean pesos in Colombia. Other methods include manipulating trade documents, and using criminal proceeds to buy gems or precious metals. Trade-based schemes are also used by informal value transfer systems to settle accounts.[16]

### *Strategy*

*Law enforcement will use all available means to identify and dismantle trade-based money laundering schemes. This strategy includes infiltrating criminal organizations to expose complex schemes from the inside, and deploying ICE-led Trade Transparency Units that facilitate the exchange and analysis of trade data among trading partners.*

### *Action Items*

- ICE will work with countries that have expressed interest in establishing Trade Transparency Units (TTUs) with the United States. ICE, with the support of the Department of State, has established TTUs in Argentina, Paraguay, Brazil, and Colombia, and is working with the governments of Mexico, the Philippines, and Malaysia to establish TTUs. The mission of a TTU is to analyze cross-border trade data in order to identify anomalies that might indicate trade-based money laundering, such as the BMPE. With Treasury Department support for domestic TTU operations, ICE conducts investigations and prosecutions related to trade-based money laundering and other financial crimes in the United States and abroad.

- Treasury and ICE will investigate how Foreign Trade Zones (FTZ), known as free trade zones outside of the United States, are abused for trade-based money laundering and will work with host nations to close this vulnerability. Operating in an FTZ allows manufacturers legal options to defer, reduce, or even eliminate U.S. customs duties. These zones are intended to promote manufacturing, but also facilitate money laundering when false documentation is used to misrepresent imports and exports.

- The United States will attack both the onshore and offshore components of the BMPE. Federal law enforcement agencies and the Department of State will work cooperatively and collaboratively with foreign law enforcement authorities to shut down the international BMPE network. In addition, U.S. Federal law enforcement agencies and offices of the Treasury will continue to work with the U.S. financial services and trade communities to raise awareness of trade-based money laundering strategies, including the BMPE.

- NDIC will dedicate analytic resources to producing a database that will collect BMPE-related data and will publish an intelligence product addressing a reverse BMPE scheme, known as *reintegro*, which is believed to account for a significant percentage of illicit proceeds laundered through the BMPE annually. When goods are exported from Colombia, the shipper must obtain documentation that allows the goods to be exported and payment to be received into the shipper's bank account. This is known as a *reintegro*, which means ''reintegrate papers.'' After the initial use of the export documents by the shipper, these papers are often sold for others to use, which can create opportunities for money laundering.[17]

---

[16] For more information on trade-based money laundering and U.S. countermeasures see Appendix A.

[17] For more information on reintegro, see: "Law Enforcement Efforts to Combat International Money Laundering Through Black Market Peso Brokering," House of Representatives Subcommittee on General Oversight and Investigations, Committee on Banking and Financial Services, U.S. House of Representatives, October 22, 1997, at:
http://commdocs.house.gov/committees/bank/hba44337.000/hba44337_0f.htm.

Goal 5:

# PROMOTE TRANSPARENCY IN THE OWNERSHIP OF LEGAL ENTITIES

*Threats and Vulnerabilities*

The organization and registration of certain business entities, such as corporations, limited liability companies, and trusts can be accomplished in all State jurisdictions with minimal public disclosure of personal information regarding controlling interests and ownership. The current lack of transparency prevents financial institutions from identifying suspicious transactions and hinders law enforcement investigations and prosecutions. Using a State-registered business entity as a front is one way that money launderers gain access to U.S. banks and other domestic financial institutions.[18]

*Strategy*

*FinCEN will enhance awareness of the misuse of legal entities for money laundering, and, with OFAC and other offices of the Treasury, will work with State administrators to explore options to increase transparency in the beneficial ownership of legal entities. FinCEN, OFAC, the IRS, and the Federal functional regulators will issue guidance on the risks of providing financial services to shell companies. Law enforcement agencies will target for prosecution individuals who use the incorporation process to facilitate money laundering.*

*Action Items*

- FinCEN, OFAC, the IRS, and the Federal functional regulators will develop guidance for financial institutions alerting them to the risks inherent in providing financial services to shell companies and other legal entities, and will suggest ways to mitigate those risks consistent with applicable AML and customer identification program regulations.

- FinCEN will publish an analytical study of the use of domestic legal entities, focusing on limited liability companies, in financial crime and money laundering.

- Offices of the Treasury, including FinCEN and OFAC, will develop and implement outreach programs with State authorities and relevant trade associations to explore legislative and administrative options to require the disclosure of ownership information in the company registration process. Outreach efforts will focus on those States with the most significant organization activity and those that are most often cited in Suspicious Activity Reports involving shell companies and other legal entities.

- The Treasury, in conjunction with FinCEN and the Federal functional regulators, will provide necessary guidance to clarify points of question about the customer identification program rule.

- The Federal Bureau of Investigation (FBI) is developing an internal working group that will focus on service providers that form companies on behalf of offshore criminal interests. The working group will identify and develop actionable leads, initiate investigations, and work cooperatively with domestic and foreign law enforcement agencies to combat threats to the United States posed by criminal organizations operating through U.S. shell companies and other legal entities.

---

[18] For more information on the money laundering threats associated with legal entities see Appendix A.

## Goal 6:
# EXAMINE ANTI-MONEY LAUNDERING REGULATORY OVERSIGHT AND ENFORCEMENT AT CASINOS

### Threats and Vulnerabilities

Casinos are a high-volume cash-intensive industry and are among a broad and varied group of nonbank financial institutions that offer money laundering opportunities outside the traditional financial services system. A number of money laundering schemes using casinos have been reported by foreign and domestic law enforcement.[19] The growth of the casino industry in recent years has been driven primarily by Native American tribes. A primary concern is to ensure that tribal gaming commissions understand their BSA compliance responsibilities.

### Strategy

*FinCEN and the IRS will develop an aggressive outreach and supervisory campaign to reach as broadly as possible across the expanding universe of casinos to enforce established AML programmatic, reporting, and recordkeeping requirements. The law enforcement community will work through the Indian Gaming Working Group (IGWG), led by the FBI, to monitor tribal casinos for criminal conduct.*

### Action Items

- FinCEN will leverage Federal supervision and enforcement resources by working with State and Tribal authorities to harmonize regulatory obligations, share information, and coordinate enforcement actions.

- FinCEN, in conjunction with the IRS, will enhance outreach to the Native American casino regulatory community to ensure the Native American tribes that own casinos fully implement the applicable BSA requirements, and to alert the sector to money laundering and terrorist financing indicators.

- FinCEN and the IRS will continue to implement a revised examination methodology to identify potentially non-compliant casinos. This new approach incorporates input from the casinos themselves, other regulators, and here law enforcement.[20]

- The FBI will continue to lead the IGWG to identify investigative priorities and allocate resources for investigations of Tribal casinos. The IGWG consists of representatives from the FBI's financial crimes, public corruption, and organized crime programs as well as representatives from other Federal agencies.

---

[19] For more information on money laundering using casinos see Appendix A.

[20] The IRS Tax Exempt and Government Entities – Office of Indian Tribal Governments is responsible for: (1) identifying all Tribal casinos subject to BSA regulation; (2) conducting and documenting BSA outreach; (3) maintaining a compliance database; and (4) assisting IRS SB/SE BSA with Tribal protocol issues and BSA examination case selection. The IRS SB/SE BSA unit is responsible for conducting BSA examinations of Tribal casinos.

## Goal 7:

# IMPLEMENT AND ENFORCE ANTI-MONEY LAUNDERING REGULATIONS FOR THE INSURANCE INDUSTRY

### *Threats and Vulnerabilities:*

Insurance companies are among a broad class of nonbank financial service providers that offer a wide variety of financial products. In addition to traditional insurance policies, insurers today also market savings and investment products and tax planning services. These various financial products and services can offer criminals opportunities for money laundering.[21] A number of money laundering methods have been used to exploit insurance products, primarily life insurance policies and annuities.

### *Strategy*

*Regulatory, supervisory, and law enforcement agencies will coordinate to enforce regulations that extend AML programmatic, reporting, and recordkeeping requirements to the insurance industry.*

### *Action Items*

- FinCEN will provide outreach and training to the insurance industry to advise on the implementation of two recent regulations regarding BSA compliance obligations. Under the new rules, certain U.S. insurance companies are required to establish AML programs and file SARs. The final rules apply to insurance companies that issue or underwrite certain products that present an increased risk for money laundering and other illicit activity.

- FinCEN, in conjunction with the Federal banking regulators, will provide guidance on the application of the recent insurance rules to banking organizations that underwrite or sell insurance products and are already subject to BSA compliance obligations under the banking laws.

- OFAC will work with State regulators and the National Association of Insurance Commissioners to promote detection and prevention of money laundering schemes that may involve violations of U.S. trade and economic sanctions.

- IRS SB/SE BSA will work to sign an information-sharing MOU with State insurance regulators. The MOU provides both the IRS and the participating State the opportunity to leverage resources for BSA examinations, training, and outreach. FinCEN and the IRS are also developing examiner training materials.

---

[21] For more information on money laundering using insurance products and U.S. countermeasures see Appendix A.

## Goal 8:

# SUPPORT GLOBAL ANTI-MONEY LAUNDERING CAPACITY BUILDING AND ENFORCEMENT EFFORTS

*Threats and Vulnerabilities:*

Countries with lax AML regulation and enforcement pose a national security threat to the United States by providing a safe haven for criminal enterprise. New payment and communications technologies are opening up the world to transnational crime and creating new options for cross-border funds transfers.

*Strategy*

*The United States will work to detect, disrupt, dismantle, and defeat money laundering networks globally by promoting transparency in the international financial system and encouraging cooperation and coordination among diplomatic, financial, and law enforcement authorities. The United States will provide education, training, and support for countries seeking to protect themselves from money laundering and will work against countries that facilitate money laundering.*

*Action Items*

- U.S. law enforcement agencies will continue to devote resources to training foreign counterparts in the investigation of sophisticated money laundering methods. Transnational crime presents a growing challenge to the U.S. law enforcement community, requiring support from investigators and law enforcement agencies worldwide that understand modern crime fighting techniques.

- DEA, through its co-chairmanship of the International Drug Enforcement Conference (IDEC), a forum of 57 countries represented by the senior drug enforcement official for each country, will implement, through the IDEC, a global money flow strategy designed to identify and attack the flow of illegal drug money as it transits the globe from countries of drug abuse to countries of drug supply and bank secrecy havens.

- ICE, through its 56 international attaches, will continue to provide technical assistance and investigative support to foreign counterparts to facilitate international investigations into money laundering, bulk cash smuggling, and other transnational financial crimes.

- FinCEN will assist in the development of financial intelligence units that will receive, analyze, and disseminate financial intelligence to domestic law enforcement and share financial information with foreign counterparts.

- The Departments of the Treasury, State, Justice, and Homeland Security, the Federal functional regulators, and the law enforcement community, will work bilaterally, regionally, and through multilateral organizations, in support of the Financial Action Task Force (FATF) 40 Recommendations and Nine Special Recommendations for preventing money laundering and terrorist financing.

- The Department of State will continue to design, coordinate, and support efforts to develop comprehensive AML regimes globally, regionally, and bilaterally with the interagency community and through multilateral organizations including the United Nations Global Programme Against Money Laundering, the Organization of American States, the Pacific Islands Forum, and the FATF-Style Regional Bodies.

- The Federal bank regulators will continue to provide training and technical assistance to foreign bank supervisory officials for the development of AML compliance programs and program supervision.

- The Treasury, in consultation with the Departments of State and Justice, and other agencies as appropriate, will use Section 311 of the USA PATRIOT Act to safeguard our financial system from foreign money laundering threats. Under this authority, U.S. financial institutions may be required to take one or more special measures when dealing with a foreign jurisdiction, financial institution, class of transaction, or type of account designated to be of primary money laundering concern.

- In conjunction with the National Strategy to Internationalize Efforts against Kleptocracy, launched in August 2006, the U.S. Government will employ its tools and authorities to target, trace, seize, and forfeit assets misappropriated by current and former senior foreign government or political officials, their close associates, and immediate family members or other politically exposed persons and deny them access to the international financial system.

- The Treasury, in collaboration with the Department of State, the Federal banking regulators, and other agencies as appropriate, will work directly with the private sector on AML program implementation in regions of global strategic significance. This initiative complements the development and implementation of jurisdictional AML controls.

- The Treasury will continue working closely with the International Monetary Fund (IMF) and the World Bank Group to promote member country programs against money laundering and will continue to help guide improvements through targeted technical assistance both directly and through the IMF and World Bank. By the end of 2005, the IMF and World Bank had conducted more than 50 assessments of member countries' compliance with the standards of the FATF and had provided technical assistance on related projects in more than 125 countries. The Treasury is also working with the multilateral development banks to strengthen their internal controls, and is encouraging the regional development banks to carry out internal risk assessments similar to those undertaken by the World Bank.

Goal 9:

# IMPROVE HOW WE MEASURE OUR PROGRESS

## Threats and Vulnerabilities

Measuring the scope of the money laundering threat and the effectiveness of law enforcement and regulatory countermeasures remains a challenge. There are no objective, quantitative benchmarks that provide a starting point because of the unreported volume of financial crime. All efforts to quantify the problem are estimates. [22]

## Strategy

*Traditional measures of our effectiveness against money laundering, such as the volume of seized or forfeited assets, indictments, and BSA filings, although imperfect, do offer useful information and are indicators of the progress the United States is making against money laundering. The United States must work toward more effectively identifying and connecting criminal activity, illicit cash, money laundering methods, cases, and outcomes.*

## Action Items

- OCDETF will support the compilation of money laundering prosecution statistics by providing data contained in its management information system regarding results achieved in OCDETF designated cases. OCDETF collects data on 14 primary money laundering activity categories to evaluate the program's progress toward attacking the financial infrastructure of major drug trafficking organizations. These 14 categories cover the most prevalent and sophisticated money laundering methods used by major drug trafficking organizations.

- ICE will compile investigative data, using the Treasury Enforcement Communications System (TECS II), which serves as the ICE investigative database for case management. TECS II contains data relating to transnational and cross-border financial crimes, including bulk cash smuggling violations, cases involving failure to file a Report of International Transportation of Currency or Monetary Instruments (CMIR)[23], and money laundering cases.

- FinCEN and other offices of the Treasury will work with the Federal law enforcement community to develop a process to evaluate and report on law enforcement's use of BSA reporting in their investigations. This information will provide meaningful feedback to the financial community on the value of this information to law enforcement, and will assist institutions in the enhancement of their AML and Suspicious Activity Reporting programs.

---

[22] The FATF Mutual Evaluation Report (MER) of the United States, supra note 1 and accompanying text, measures the U.S. AML/CFT regime against the FATF 40 Recommendations and 9 Special Recommendations and is a significant benchmark of the effectiveness of the U.S AML/CFT system. .

[23] 31 U.S.C. 5316 requires individuals to report the transport or transfer of more than $10,000 in currency or monetary instruments into or out of the United States.

# LIST OF APPENDICES

Appendix A – U.S. Money Laundering Threat Assessment

Appendix B – Money Laundering Statistics

Appendix C – Law Enforcement Data and Intelligence Centers

Appendix D – Strategic Use of Asset Forfeiture

# Appendix A: U.S. Money Laundering Threat Assessment

# INTRODUCTION

The 2005 Money Laundering Threat Assessment (MLTA) is the first government-wide analysis of money laundering in the United States. The report is the product of an interagency working group composed of experts from the spectrum of U.S. Government agencies, bureaus, and offices that study and combat money laundering. The purpose of the MLTA is to help policy makers, regulators, and the law enforcement community better understand the landscape of money laundering in the United States and to support strategic planning efforts to combat money laundering.

The working group synthesized law enforcement statistics and observations, regulatory data (such as Bank Secrecy Act filings), private sector studies, and public information to assess the vulnerabilities that allow criminals to launder money through particular money laundering methods or conduits.

The MLTA offers a detailed analysis of thirteen money laundering methods, ranging from well-established techniques for integrating dirty money into the financial system to modern innovations that exploit global payment networks as well as the Internet. Each chapter focuses on a specific money laundering method and provides a brief overview of the methodology, an assessment of vulnerabilities – including geographic or other noted concentrations – and the regulatory/public policy backdrop.

While not exhaustive, the assessment consolidates a tremendous amount of information and insight contributed by the various participating agencies as to the major methods of money laundering that they confront. The overall picture is both sobering and promising. The volume of dirty money circulating through the United States is undeniably vast and criminals are enjoying new advantages with globalization and the advent of new financial services such as stored value cards and online payment systems. At the same time, there has been considerable progress. The approach of U.S. law enforcement and regulatory agencies has undergone a sea change over the past decade, such that money laundering is now treated as an independent and primary focus across all relevant agencies. With this change in approach and focus have come marked improvements in both systemic and applied anti-money laundering

(AML) efforts. Most encouraging are interagency initiatives and task forces that, when properly coordinated, bring the talents, expertise, and resources of multiple agencies to bear on a problem to great effect. With so many agencies looking at distinct but related aspects of this issue, it is critical that information be shared freely and studied jointly. Highlighted below are some notable examples of recent U.S. agency advances in organization, analysis, and execution in the fight against money laundering:

U.S. Immigration and Customs Enforcement (ICE), has introduced many new initiatives aimed at analyzing and combating the movement of illicit funds by bulk cash smuggling, trade-based money laundering, courier hubs, money services businesses (MSBs), charities, and alternative remittance systems. These initiatives include:

- Operation Cornerstone, founded in 2003 – a private industry partnership and aggressive outreach program;

- A Trade Transparency Unit (TTU) aimed at identifying anomalies related to cross-border trade indicative of money laundering;

- A multi-agency approach (in partnership with Internal Revenue Service – Criminal Investigation (IRS-CI), FinCEN, and the Federal Bureau of Investigation (FBI)) to target unlicensed MSBs; and

- A Foreign Political Corruption Task Force in Miami to address foreign public corruption and related money laundering.

With respect to bulk cash smuggling in particular, ICE is:

- Working with Customs and Border Protection (CBP) to share training and expertise with the Mexican government as to how to execute successful bulk cash smuggling interdiction operations;

- Providing training in bulk cash smuggling interdiction to 28 developing countries in the Middle East, South America, Africa, and Asia, in concert with CBP and the State Department; and

- Conducting training in bulk cash smuggling interdiction, funded by the Executive Office for Organized Crime Drug Enforcement Task Forces (OCDETF), in seven major cities throughout the United States, attended by federal, state and local law enforcement.

The FBI is working to develop advanced technologies to exploit Suspicious Activity Reports (SARs) and other Bank Secrecy Act (BSA) data from FinCEN by using computer software to visualize financial patterns, link distinct criminal activities, and display the activity in link analysis charts. The FBI is also implementing a next-generation electronic file management system that will help manage investigative, administrative, and intelligence needs while also improving ways to encourage information sharing with other agencies.

The Administrator of the Drug Enforcement Administration (DEA) issued a directive in 2003 restoring DEA's primary focus to the financial aspects of drug investigations. Currently, every DEA investigation includes a financial component. DEA also undertook the following steps to promote this focus:

- Established an Office of Financial Operations;

- Established specialized money laundering groups in every DEA Field Division, and increased Special Agent resources devoted to money laundering invstigations in key foreign offices;

- Created and presented specialized money laundering training to DEA agents and analysts;

- Established a "Bulk Currency Initiative" to coordinate all U.S. highway money seizures for the purpose of developing the evidence necessary to identify, disrupt, and dismantle large-scale narcotics trafficking organizations; and

- Initiated a global money flow study, through its position as chair of the International Drug Enforcement Conference, to identify and target drug proceeds flowing from countries of drug abuse to countries of drug supply.

The IRS, as part of its core tax administration mission, addresses both the criminal and civil aspects of money laundering. IRS-CI special agents "follow the money"

within various inter-agency task forces and centers. IRS-CI also has 41 active Suspicious Activity Report Review Teams (SAR-RT) reviewing and analyzing SAR data for case development and support throughout the country. Recently-acquired "data mining" software is improving the ability of IRS-CI's investigators and analysts to make connections and identify patterns in the SAR data.

On the civil side, the IRS established a new organization within its Small Business/Self-employed (SB/SE) Division, the Office of Fraud/BSA, which has end-to-end accountability for BSA oversight of certain non-bank financial institutions. There are over 300 examiners and managers who are fully trained and dedicated full-time to the BSA program. The IRS has also completed a model Federal/State Memorandum of Understanding which provides both IRS and the participating state the opportunity to leverage resources for BSA examinations, outreach, and training.

Treasury's Office of Terrorist Financing and Financial Crime (TFFC), a part of the Office of Terrorism and Financial Intelligence, is working to develop and drive anti-money laundering policy and initiatives at home and abroad. A primary initiative of this office is to lead the interagency development of the *National Money Laundering Strategy*. In crafting this and other strategies, TFFC works with the law enforcement, regulatory, and intelligence communities, in addition to the private sector and overseas counterparts, to identify and address systemic vulnerabilities. In addition, TFFC, along with inter-agency counterparts, has been a driving force behind the worldwide propagation of strong anti-money laundering standards via the Financial Action Task Force (FATF), the preeminent international body on money laundering issues. Over the past two years, scores of new countries – from North Africa to the Persian Gulf region to Eurasia – have joined FATF-style regional bodies, such that over 150 nations have now committed themselves to adopting FATF's standards and to being evaluated against them.

The BSA, administered by the Treasury Department's Financial Crimes Enforcement Network (FinCEN), is the cornerstone of the U.S. Government's AML framework and was recently expanded in scope and depth. Today, businesses under the BSA umbrella include casinos, jewelers, MSBs (such as check cashers and money transmitters), securities dealers, and others.

FinCEN is itself undergoing a broad transformation. The bureau is changing the way it analyzes information, moving away from functioning simply as a clearinghouse, and moving towards higher-level research and analysis, which will utilize all sources of information to analyze the cutting-edge systems of money laundering and illicit finance. FinCEN has also signed memoranda of understanding with the federal regulatory agencies that have received delegated authority from FinCEN to examine financial institutions for compliance with the BSA. The goal is better coordination and communication leading to effective implementation and enforcement of the BSA, which ultimately should help to achieve a sustained and successful attack on money laundering in the United States.

The U.S. Postal Inspection Service (USPIS) enjoys the advantage of having more than 100,000 postal clerks and managers on the alert for possible suspicious activity. These employees file over 500 SARs per week to the U.S. Postal Service (USPS) BSA Compliance Office. USPIS recently established an Intelligence Analysis Unit (IAU) at its headquarters office to ensure that these reports as well as back room analysis are being utilized effectively. The IAU methodically analyzes the USPS BSA database, searching for clues that might indicate major money laundering operations and possible terrorist financing schemes. The IAU both responds to investigative inquiries from field inspectors and proactively initiates investigative leads for the field.

The Department of Justice's Asset Forfeiture and Money Laundering Section (AFMLS) reports that the USA PATRIOT Act provided a number of new tools to identify and track criminal proceeds. Section 319(a) has been of particular importance, allowing the government to capture criminal assets held abroad if the criminal proceeds are deposited in a foreign bank that maintains a correspondent account in the United States. The Civil Asset Reform Act of 2000 is another important tool assisting federal law enforcement in making asset forfeitures. The law makes possible both the criminal and civil forfeiture of the proceeds of all specified unlawful activities. Many U.S. Attorney's Offices will not approve an indictment for presentation to the grand jury until a forfeiture specialist has reviewed it for possible criminal forfeiture

and/or the filing of a parallel civil forfeiture complaint.

In 2005, the Departments of Justice, Homeland Security,[1] and Treasury established a multi-agency drug and financial intelligence fusion center through the OCDETF program. Leads resulting from the efforts of the Fusion Center will support the initiation and development of coordinated international, national, and regional investigations. AFMLS, in partnership with OCDETF, has conducted Financial Investigation Training Seminars in every OCDETF region in the country during the past two years.

The National Drug Intelligence Center (NDIC), whose mission is to develop strategic domestic drug intelligence, created a Money Laundering Unit in January 2005 to provide a multi-source fusion capability for money laundering-related information. The mission of this unit is to identify strategic money laundering trends and patterns for national policy makers.

The Treasury Executive Office for Asset Forfeiture (TEOAF) administers the Treasury Forfeiture Fund, and has implemented a strategic focus on promoting "high impact cases," or cases that generate $100,000 or more in forfeited value. In FY 2004, the Fund received more than $335 million in revenue, 84% of which was derived from "high impact cases." TEOAF then uses this money to fund law enforcement training, special programs, and criminal investigations.

Legal, structural, and strategic advances improve the ability of U.S. agencies to track and combat money launderers. That said, money laundering remains a massive and evolving challenge that will require clear, strategic thinking. Measuring the problem is an essential first step. Studies have traditionally looked to that portion of illicit activity that is apprehended by authorities as an indicator of the types of money laundering going on and trends within the field. Such indicators include seized or forfeited assets, indictments, and BSA filings

---

[1] The United States Coast Guard.

by financial institutions, such as SARs. Each of these is admittedly imperfect, but could offer much useful information.

Unfortunately, however, the data are not as developed as they should be and not collected in a systematic way across the U.S. government. It is currently not possible, for example, to quantify with accuracy the total amount of money laundering activity being apprehended by federal law enforcement agencies, let alone state and local law enforcement. Individual tracking systems developed and tailored to meet particular agency priorities and needs have yielded often incompatible systems. Problems include data fields that are collected by some but not all agencies, disparities in definitions, and redundancies wherein two or more agencies log the same seizure or arrest because the case was handled through a joint task force. Agencies may not even share common definitions of what constitutes "money laundering proceeds," or what nexus to the United States warrants defining illicit activity as "United States" money laundering.

Appendices to this assessment make the most of the existing data to offer a rough quantitative analysis of money laundering concentrations. Going forward, though, more data needs to be collected in a more consistent way across agencies. Of particular importance is information that would track, with respect to every money laundering seizure, the following: (1) the predicate crime, (2) the money laundering method/s utilized, and (3) the source and suspected destination of the proceeds. Accurate, comprehensive data is vitally important if we are to assess whether we are collectively gaining ground, keeping pace, or falling behind criminal money launderers in each of the various methodologies that they employ.

## Chapter 1
# BANKING

Banks and other depository financial institutions in the United States are unique in that they alone are allowed to engage in the business of receiving deposits and providing direct access to those deposits through the payments system. The payments system encompasses paper checks and various electronic payment networks facilitating credit and debit cards and bank-to-bank transfers. The unique role banks play makes them the first line of defense against money laundering.

Depository financial institutions (DFIs), which include commercial banks, savings and loan associations (also called thrifts), and credit unions form the financial backbone of the United States.[2] Although Money Service Businesses (MSBs) may offer an alternative to banks, MSBs must themselves engage the services of a DFI to hold deposits, clear checks, and settle transactions. Thus in almost every money laundering typology, a bank is employed domestically or abroad to hold or move funds. The stage at which funds are introduced into the banking system is a critical one. A report from the New York Clearing House, which operates bank payment systems, acknowledges: "Once a person is able to inject funds into the payment system that are a product of a criminal act or are intended to finance a criminal act, it is highly difficult, and in many cases impossible, to identify those funds as they move from bank to bank."[3]

The BSA requires banks to establish and maintain effective anti-money laundering (AML) programs, implement customer identification programs, and maintain transaction records. Banks also are obligated to report cash transactions exceeding $10,000 as well as transactions that appear suspicious.

Banks are ubiquitous in the United States but industry consolidation, due to deregulation and competitive pres-

sures, is reducing the number of distinct DFIs. At year end in 2004 there were, for the first time since the FDIC was created in 1934, fewer than 9,000 federally-insured commercial banks and savings institutions in the United States, not including credit unions.[4]

Another significant development in the banking sector is the ongoing decline in the use of paper checks. By 2003, for the first time, most payments not made by cash were made electronically, though it takes all forms of electronic payments combined to rival the number of checks paid. Previously, paper checks ranked right behind cash as the most favored form of payment. By the end of the decade, the Federal Reserve predicts credit and debit card payments will each surpass check volume.[5]

The shift from paper to electronic payments is changing the economics of the payments business putting emphasis on lowering costs. In response, banks are increasingly using the Internet as a means for customers to open or access accounts.[6] Moving away from face-to-face customer interaction, particularly for account openings, challenges the traditional process of customer due diligence. Similarly, the steady influx of immigrants without U.S. Government-issued identification is requiring banks to explore new ways to verify the identity of their customers.

Despite the rapid growth in electronic payments and the accelerating pace of change in financial services, domestic payment networks in countries around the world do not connect with one another. A bank in the United States cannot transmit a payment directly to a foreign bank unless the U.S. bank has a presence in the foreign country. That presence can be either an overseas branch of the U.S. bank or a correspondent account. A bank chartered in a foreign country faces the same option if it wants to provide services in the United States for its customers. Instead of bearing the costs of licensing, staffing, and operating its own offices in the United States,

---

[2]  The term "bank" will be used generically in this chapter to refer to all forms of DFI.

[3]  Guidelines for Counter Money Laundering Policies and Procedures in Correspondent Banking, sponsored by the New York Clearing House Association, LLC, March 2002.

[4]  FDIC Quarterly Banking Profile, Fourth Quarter 2004. Accessed at: http://www2.fdic.gov/qbp/2004dec/qbp.pdf.

[5]  The 2004 Federal Reserve Payments Study, December 15, 2004.

[6]  Saranow, Jennifer, Banks Speed Process for Opening Online Accounts, Wall Street Journal, Feb. 3, 2005.

the bank can open a correspondent account with a U.S. bank.[7] According to a Congressional report on money laundering and correspondent banking: "Today, banks establish multiple correspondent relationships throughout the world in order to engage in international financial transactions for themselves and their clients in places where they do not have a physical presence. Many of the largest international banks serve as correspondents for thousands of other banks."[8]

## Vulnerabilities

Banks, although obligated to implement a customer identification program, must contend with businesses and consumers who may attempt to disguise their true identity and source of income. Cash-intensive businesses, for example, may inflate how much legitimate cash comes in each day to disguise the deposit of cash from illegal drug sales or other criminal activity. Banks attempt to spot these deceptions at the point accounts are opened or to recognize suspicious deposit and withdrawal activity as it occurs.

As banks venture into opening accounts online and providing online account access, it becomes increasingly difficult to verify customer identification. The move away from face-to-face account opening and account access creates opportunities for fraud and identity theft. Unauthorized access to checking accounts is the fastest growing form of identity theft. In October 2005, the Federal Financial Institutions Examination Council (FFIEC), a body composed of the DFI federal regulatory agencies, issued industry guidance titled: Authentication in an Internet Banking Environment. The document advises financial institutions offering Internet-based products and services to use customer authentication techniques "appropriate to those products and services."[9] According to HSBC, banks may be forced to restrict online access only to customers with appropriate hardware and/or software.[10]

In addition to the difficulty financial institutions face identifying their customers online, the growing adoption of electronic payment systems is producing new opportunities for electronic fraud.[11] New forms of electronic funds transfers, including Internet- and telephone-initiated payments, and the conversion at the point-of-sale of paper checks to electronic debits, all use the automated clearinghouse (ACH), an electronic payment network designed for bank-to-bank transactions rather than for direct access by consumers and businesses.[12] More than 12 billion ACH payments were made in 2004, a 20 percent increase over 2003.[13] Consumers initiated almost one billion ACH payments via the Internet, worth more than $300 billion last year, which was a 40.4 percent increase over 2003.[14]

A major vulnerability the BSA attempts to address is foreigners sending and receiving payments through U.S. banks using "correspondent," "payable through," or "nested" accounts, which, without adequate due diligence, can shield the payer's true identity. The farther removed an individual or entity is from the bank, the more difficult it is to verify the identity of the customer. Correspondent accounts and "payable through" accounts streamline cross-border transactions but create opportunities to use a U.S. or foreign bank without the bank knowing the true payment originator. A "payable through" account at a U.S. bank would, for example, involve a foreign bank holding a checking account at the U.S. institution. The foreign bank could then issue checks to its customers allowing them to write checks on the U.S. account. A foreign bank may have several hundred customers writing checks on one "payable through" account, and all are considered signatories on the account at the U.S. bank.

---

[7] Minority Staff of the Permanent Subcommittee on Investigations Report on Correspondent Banking: A Gateway for Money Laundering, February 5, 2001.

[8] *Ibid.*

[9] FFIEC, Authentication in an Internet Banking Environment. Accessed at: http://www.ffiec.gov/pdf/authentication_guidance.pdf.

[10] Goodwin, Bill, *HSBC Warns Of Online Banking Bans*, Computerweekly.com, April 12, 2005. Accessed at: http://www.computerweekly.com/articles/article.asp?liArticleID=137822&liArticleTypeID=1&liCategoryID=6&liChannelID=22&liFlavourID=1&sSearch=&nPage=1#.

[11] Putting an End to Account-Hijacking Identity Theft, FDIC, Division of Supervision and Consumer Protection Technology Supervision Branch, December 14, 2004.

[12] The ACH was designed for low value recurring transactions, specifically direct deposit of payroll and monthly consumer bill payments that remain the same each month.

[13] The National Automated Clearing House Association. Accessed at: http://www.nacha.org/.

[14] *Ibid.*

A variation on the "payable through" account is "nesting," in which foreign banks open correspondent accounts at U.S. banks but then solicit other foreign banks to use the account. Nested accounts provide indirect access to the U.S. financial system by allowing a foreign bank that does not have a direct correspondent relationship with a U.S. financial institution to use another bank's U.S. correspondent account. These second-tier foreign banks then solicit individuals as customers. This results in an exponential increase in the number of individuals having signatory authority over a single account at a U.S. banking entity.

Of particular concern are foreign "shell banks" – foreign banks that do not maintain a physical presence in any country – that seek to access the U.S. financial system via correspondent accounts.

### Cash Letter/Pouch Activity[15]

As cross border wire transfers come under increased scrutiny and regulation, criminals have found paper checks, money orders, and cashier's checks to be an effective method to move money internationally. These more traditional payment instruments take a longer time to clear when traveling outside the United States but are perceived by money launderers as being subject to less scrutiny.

Money launderers can transfer large dollar amounts by writing a number of checks or buying a number of money orders at various U.S. locations, with each payment below the reporting threshold. The dollar-denominated payments are mailed or transported to accomplices overseas who deposit the checks and other payments in foreign bank accounts. Because these are dollar-denominated payments, the foreign banks that receive them send them back to the United States for deposit

in their U.S. correspondent accounts. The checks and money orders are bundled up at the foreign banks and sent with a deposit slip (referred to in the industry as a "cash letter") with the details of each check and money order. The U.S. correspondent bank credits the foreign bank's U.S. account and routes the individual payment instruments to the appropriate paying banks and other institutions.

Some banks handle as many as five to seven million checks a day delivered by shipping companies in pouches and overnight bags. Processing is done as efficiently as possible, making it very difficult to aggregate related payments or scrutinize individual payments for evidence of money laundering.

### Private Banking

Private banking is defined as "the personal or discreet offering of a wide variety of financial services and products to the affluent market. These operations typically offer all-inclusive personalized services. Individuals, commercial businesses, law firms, investment advisors, trusts, and personal investment companies may open private banking accounts."[16] Private banking relationships have proved problematic. In contrast to "nesting" or "payable through" accounts, money laundering through private banking relationships more often involves a gross failure of due diligence, if not bank complicity.

Riggs National Bank was fined over forty million dollars as a consequence of serious deficiencies in its AML program, including in its private banking practice.[17] Riggs opened multiple private banking accounts for former Chilean dictator Augusto Pinochet, among other politically exposed persons, accepting millions of dollars in deposits under various corporate and individual account names and paying little or no attention to suspicious activity in these accounts.[18] Other major banks have also

---

[15] This section is drawn from the testimony of John F. Moynihan and Larry C. Johnson, partners, BERG Associates, LLC, before the House Committee on Financial Services, Subcommittee on Oversight and Investigations, March 11, 2003.

[16] Money Laundering: A Banker's Guide to Avoiding Problems, Office of the Comptroller of the Currency, Dec, 2002. Accessed at: http://www.occ.treas.gov/moneylaundering2002.pdf.

[17] See, e.g., In the Matter of Riggs Bank, N.A., No. 2004-01, Assessment of Civil Monetary Penalty (May 13, 2004); "Money Laundering and Foreign Corruption: Enforcement and Effectiveness of the Patriot Act," Supplemental Staff Report on U.S. Accounts Used by Augusto Pinochet, U.S. Senate Permanent Subcommittee on Investigations, March 16, 2005.

[18] Guidance on applying scrutiny to situations of this type has been available for some time. See Guidance on Enhanced Scrutiny for Transactions that May Involve the Proceeds of Foreign Corruption (January 2001). Accessed at: http://www.federalreserve.gov/boarddocs/SRLETTERS/2001/sr0103a1.pdf.

come under criticism for the laxity of their private banking AML policies and procedures.[19]

In 2003, ICE established a Politically Exposed Person (PEP) Task Force in Miami to address the vulnerability of relationships between private banks and corrupt foreign officials. The PEP Task Force works with ICE field offices and foreign governments in the identification of public corruption-related proceeds laundered through U.S. financial institutions. Increasingly, Central American, South American, and Caribbean governments are seeking the assistance of the United States in developing evidence against, and locating the assets of, corrupt government officials and prominent citizens involved in the theft or embezzlement of public and private funds. ICE agents are currently investigating several cases that involve illicit funds channeled into the United States from Caribbean, Central American, South American, and Pacific Rim countries that were used to purchase assets domestically and abroad.

## Regulation and Public Policy

Under the BSA, all financial institutions must develop, administer, and maintain a program that ensures compliance with the law's reporting and recordkeeping requirements. The compliance program is tailored to a bank's business operations and risks. By law, the program must include the following four components:

- A system of internal controls to assure ongoing BSA compliance;

- Independent testing of the DFI's compliance;

- The designation of an individual responsible for coordinating and monitoring day-to-day compliance; and

- Training for appropriate personnel.[20]

Banks and certain other DFIs must implement a written customer identification program appropriate for their size, location, and type of business.[21] The program must include account-opening procedures that specify the identifying information that will be obtained from each customer, and it must include reasonable and practical risk-based procedures for verifying the customer's identity. The procedures are supposed to enable a bank to form a reasonable belief that it knows the true identity of each customer.

DFIs are required to file SARs, reporting any instances of known or suspected illegal or suspicious activity.[22] To ensure that it will be able to identify suspicious activity, a DFI should have in place a customer due diligence (CDD) program under which the organization (1) assesses the risks associated with a customer account or transaction, and (2) gathers sufficient information to evaluate whether a particular transaction warrants the filing of a SAR. In addition, appropriate systems and controls are to be in place to monitor and identify suspicious or unusual activity. CDD protocols vary depending on the activities associated with different types and volumes of banking transactions and their risk. (See Tables 1 and 2 for SAR data analysis).

The number of SARs filed by depository institutions from 1996 through 2003 increased on average by more than 25% annually.[23] The total number of suspicious activity reports filed in 2005 is projected to surpass 700,000. FinCEN indicates that some of this increase is warranted, while some may be attributed to "defensive filing" by financial institutions, in which SARs are filed on non-suspicious transactions out of concern about regulatory and criminal scrutiny. Such defensive filing dilutes the value of the information in the BSA database.[24]

Examination authority over banks and other depository institutions for BSA compliance has been delegated by

---

[19] Testimony of Herbert A. Biern, Senior Associate Director, Division of Banking Supervision and Regulation, Federal Reserve Board, before the Committee on International Relations, U.S. House of Representatives November 17, 2004.

[20] See 31 U.S.C. § 5318(h)(1).

[21] See 31 U.S.C. § 5318(l) and 31 C.F.R. § 103.121 (for banks, savings associations, credit unions, and certain non-federally regulated banks).

[22] See 31 U.S.C. § 5318(g).

[23] FinCEN, By The Numbers, Issue 3, Dec. 2004.

[24] Statement of William Fox, Director Financial Crime Enforcement Network, United States Department of the Treasury, before the United States House of Representatives Committee on Financial Services Subcommittee on Oversight and Investigations, May 26, 2005.

FinCEN to the industry's five functional regulators.[25] The federal bank regulators include a review of BSA compliance in their periodic examinations. In the second half of 2004, the federal banking regulators completed 44 public enforcement actions involving BSA violations. Among the problems most often cited was the lack of independent testing to validate BSA compliance. In about 60% of the BSA cases that were closed in the second half, a bank was ordered to arrange for testing or was cited for failure to do so.[26] Several banks in recent years have faced severe criminal and civil penalties as a consequence of BSA lapses.

In June 2005, the FFIEC released a joint BSA/AML examination manual. This manual will assist examiners in evaluating banks' BSA/AML compliance programs, regardless of the size or business lines of the bank. This manual should provide for enhanced consistency in the interpretation of BSA and AML requirements across the various agencies.

With respect to shell banks, Section 313 of the USA PATRIOT Act and its implementing regulations prohibit covered U.S. banks and broker-dealers from establishing, maintaining, administering, or managing a correspondent account for a foreign shell bank.[27] In addition, U.S. banks and broker-dealers must take reasonable measures to ensure that any correspondent account that they establish, maintain, administer, or manage for a foreign bank is not being used by the foreign bank to provide banking services indirectly to a foreign shell bank.[28]

Section 312 of the USA PATRIOT Act provides, among other things, for enhanced due diligence with respect to certain correspondent accounts held on behalf of banks operating under an offshore license and also mandates enhanced scrutiny for private banking accounts maintained for senior foreign political figures.

Finally, Section 319 requires covered financial institutions that provide correspondent accounts to foreign banks to maintain records of the foreign bank's owners and to maintain the name and address of an agent in the United States designated to accept service of legal process for the foreign bank for records regarding the correspondent account.

---

[25] The five functional regulators for the banking industry include the Board of Governors of the Federal Reserve System (Federal Reserve), the Federal Deposit Insurance Corporation, the National Credit Union Association, the Office of the Comptroller of the Currency, and the Office of Thrift Supervision. State-chartered private banks, trust companies, and credit unions without federal insurance have no federal functional regulator, and come under the purview of the IRS SB/SE Division for purposes of BSA examination.

[26] Vartanian, Thomas P., Focus on BSA, Laundering Continued; Bank Secrecy Act, American Banker, April 1, 2005.

[27] 31 U.S.C. §5318(j)(1); 31 CFR 103.177(a)(1).

[28] 31 U.S.C. §5318(j)(2); 31 CFR 103.177(a)(1).

| Rank | State/Territory | Filings (Overall) | Percentage (Overall) |
|------|-----------------|-------------------|----------------------|
| 1 | California | 351,784 | 24.26% |
| 2 | New York | 167,635 | 11.56% |
| 3 | Texas | 92,168 | 6.36% |
| 4 | Florida | 89,413 | 6.17% |
| 5 | Illinois | 51,004 | 3.52% |
| 6 | Arizona | 48,691 | 3.36% |
| 7 | New Jersey | 41,403 | 2.86% |
| 8 | Pennsylvania | 37,765 | 2.60% |
| 9 | Ohio | 34,634 | 2.39% |
| 10 | Michigan | 34,506 | 2.38% |

Table 1

*The top ten states for Suspicious Activity Report filings from depository institutions from April 1, 1996 through June 30, 2004 account for two-thirds of all SARs for the period. Source FinCEN, By The Numbers, Issue 3.*

| Violation Type | Filings (Overall) | Percentage (Overall) |
|----------------|-------------------|----------------------|
| BSA/Structuring/Money Laundering | 769,502 | 48.22% |
| Check Fraud | 185,839 | 11.65% |
| Other | 136,021 | 8.52% |
| Credit Card Fraud | 77,970 | 4.89% |
| Counterfeit Check | 74,891 | 4.69% |
| Check Kiting | 55,940 | 3.51% |
| Unknown/Blank | 46,783 | 2.93% |
| Defalcation/Embezzlement | 46,323 | 2.90% |
| Mortgage Loan Fraud | 40,016 | 2.51% |
| Consumer Loan Fraud | 27,240 | 1.71% |
| False Statement | 26,724 | 1.67% |
| Misuse of Position or Self Dealing | 18,460 | 1.16% |
| Wire Transfer Fraud | 17,634 | 1.11% |
| Mysterious Disappearance | 17,375 | 1.09% |
| Debit Card Fraud | 11,315 | Less than 1% |
| Commercial Loan Fraud | 10,699 | Less than 1% |
| Identity Theft* | 10,188 | Less than 1% |
| Computer Intrusion* | 8,319 | Less than 1% |
| Counterfeit Credit/Debit Card | 6,573 | Less than 1% |
| Counterfeit Instrument (Other) | 5,142 | Less than 1% |
| Bribery/Gratuity | 1,799 | Less than 1% |
| Terrorist Financing* | 971 | Less than 1% |

Table 2

*Suspicious Activity Reports filed by depository institutions ranked by suspicious activity, based on filings from April 1, 1996 to June 30, 2004.*

*\* The category "computer intrusion" was added June 2000 and "identity theft" and "terrorist financing" were added July 2003. Source FinCEN, By The Numbers, Issue 3.*

## Chapter 2
# MONEY SERVICES BUSINESSES

Money Services Businesses (MSBs) provide a full range of financial products and services outside of the banking system. For individuals who may not have ready access to the formal banking sector, MSBs provide a valuable service. They also pose a considerable threat. MSBs in the United States are expanding at a rapid rate, often operate without supervision, and transact business with overseas counterparts that are largely unregulated. Moreover, their services are available without the necessity of opening an account. As other financial institutions come under greater scrutiny in their implementation of and compliance with BSA requirements, MSBs have become increasingly attractive to financial criminals.

Under existing BSA regulations, MSBs are defined to include five distinct types of financial services providers (including the U.S. Postal Service (USPS)): (1) currency dealers or exchangers; (2) check cashers; (3) issuers of traveler's checks, money orders, or stored value cards; (4) sellers or redeemers of traveler's checks, money orders, or stored value; and (5) money transmitters. Because of the great variance in characteristics and vulnerabilities across the various types of MSB, the main categories of MSBs will be treated in separate subchapters below. Some introductory remarks follow that pertain to all MSBs.

With limited exceptions, MSBs are subject to the full range of BSA regulatory controls, including the AML rule, suspicious activity and currency transaction reporting rules, and various other identification and recordkeeping rules.[29] Additionally, existing BSA regulations require certain MSB principals to register with the Treasury Department.[30] Federal regulations contain a definitional threshold for all MSBs except for money transmitters: A business that engages in MSB-type transactions will be considered an MSB only if it conducts more than $1,000 of transactions in a particular category of money services transactions for any person on any day (in one or more transactions).[31] Finally, many states have established AML supervisory requirements that are often incorporated into the requirement that an MSB be licensed with the state in which it is incorporated or does business.

Many MSBs, including the vast majority of money transmitters in the United States, operate through a system of agents. While agents are not presently required to register, they are themselves MSBs that are required to establish AML programs and comply with the other recordkeeping and reporting requirements described above. A 1997 Coopers & Lybrand study (Coopers Study) estimated that approximately eight business enterprises, through a system of agents, accounted for the bulk of MSB financial products offered within the United States and the bulk of locations at which these financial products were offered. This group comprises large firms with significant capitalization that are publicly traded on major securities exchanges. A larger group of, on average, far smaller enterprises competes with the largest firms in a highly bifurcated market for

---

[29] *See* 31 CFR 103.125 (requirement for money services businesses to establish and maintain an anti-money laundering program); 31 CFR 103.22 (requirement for money services businesses to file currency transaction reports); 31 CFR 103.20 (requirement for money services businesses to file suspicious activity reports, other than for check cashing and stored value transactions); 31 CFR 103.29 (requirement for money services businesses that sell money orders, traveler's checks, or other instruments for cash to verify the identity of the customer and create and maintain a record of each cash purchase between $3,000 and $10,000, inclusive); 31 CFR 103.33(f) and (g) (rules applicable to certain transmittals of funds); and 31 CFR 103.37 (additional recordkeeping requirement for currency exchangers including the requirement to create and maintain a record of each exchange of currency in excess of $1,000).

[30] *See* 31 CFR 103.41. The registration requirement applies to all money services businesses (whether or not licensed as a money services business by any state) except the U.S. Postal Service; agencies of the United States, of any state, or of any political subdivision of a state; issuers, sellers, or redeemers of stored value, or any person that is a money services business solely because that person serves as an agent of another money services business (however, a money services business that engages in activities described in § 103.11(uu) both on its own behalf and as an agent for others is required to register).

[31] *See* 31 CFR 103.11(uu).

money services.[32] These small enterprises may own only one location with two to four employees, and may provide both financial services and unrelated services or products.[33] Less is known about this second tier of firms than about the major providers of money service products.

Based on the Coopers Study, FinCEN estimated the number of MSBs nationwide in 1997 to be in excess of 200,000. A majority of the MSB population is made up of agents of the major businesses (*e.g.*, Western Union and MoneyGram). Additionally, in 1997, approximately 40,000 MSBs were outlets of the USPS, which sells money orders.

Outside of the major firms, rates of registration with Treasury have remained low. Despite repeated outreach efforts to the sector, only a small fraction of the total MSBs – around 23,000 – have registered with the federal government.[34] FinCEN notes that small MSBs are largely aware of the pertinent regulations but fail to register because of language, culture, cost, and training issues.

## Vulnerabilities

The fleeting nature of the customer's relationship with an MSB is a significant vulnerability. In contrast to banks, one does not need to be an existing "customer" of an MSB and a customer can repeatedly use different MSBs to transact business. This makes customer due diligence very difficult.

MSBs are used at all stages of the money laundering process. A review of SARs filed[35] by MSBs from October 1, 2002 through December 31, 2004 shows that money laundering and structuring represented the most frequently reported suspicious activity, cited in over 73% of MSB SARs filed. These reports point most

commonly to customers attempting to evade the $3,000 funds transfer recordkeeping requirement (or the $3,000 recordkeeping requirement for cash purchases of money orders or traveler's checks) by either breaking up a large transaction into smaller transactions or by spreading transactions out over two or more customers.

OCDETF identifies MSBs as an increasingly-prevalent conduit for laundering illicit proceeds. From 2002 to 2004, OCDETF saw a 5 percent increase in MSB-related cases, with the proportion of total money laundering cases growing from 11% to 16%.

FBI field offices consistently identified MSBs as the third-most utilized money laundering method that they encounter, after formal banking systems and cash businesses, and particularly pointed to money remitters as a threat. MSBs co-located with convenience stores

---

**CASE EXAMPLE 1**

Layering through MSBs

SDNY-2002- An individual defendant laundered more than $700,000 worth of drug proceeds for a money laundering group associated with Colombian narcotics traffickers. The defendant wired funds to bank accounts in Panama, Barbados, and Honduras. As part of the defendant's money laundering scheme, between November 1998 and June 2000, he made structured cash purchases of money orders totaling more than $600,000 without ever causing a Currency Transaction Report (CTR) report to be filed. On more than 50 occasions, the defendant made multiple small purchases of postal money orders at various post office locations, as many as 11 on a single day, keeping them below the $3,000 recordkeeping threshold. The defendant completed the money orders in his name, the name of his company, and the names of relatives and friends, and then deposited the money orders into his company's business bank account. The defendant also exchanged more than $500,000 worth of what he understood was drug money for checks from various business accomplices, including numerous carpet dealers. This activity was determined to have been an intentional circumvention of federal reporting requirements.

---

[32] For example, according to the Coopers study, at the time of that study, two money transmitters and two traveler's check issuers made up approximately 97 percent of their respective known markets for non-bank money services. Three enterprises made up approximately 88 per cent of the $100 billion in money orders sold annually (through approximately 146,000 locations). The retail foreign currency exchange sector was found by Coopers & Lybrand to be somewhat less concentrated, with the top two non-bank market participants accounting for 40 per cent of a known market that accounts for $10 billion. Check cashing is the least concentrated of the business sectors; the two largest non-bank check cashing businesses make up approximately 20 per cent of the market, with a large number of competitors.

[33] Members of the second group may include, for example, a travel agency, courier service, convenience store, grocery or liquor store.

[34] It is not known how many unregistered MSBs exist that require registration. The 1997 Coopers Study estimate of 200,000 included all MSBs, and is not indicative of the number of MSBs requiring registration.

[35] More than one violation may be identified on a single SAR.

and gas stations were cited as the most common sites for money laundering, with travel agencies that offer MSB services also noted as an increasingly prominent conduit for the illicit transmission of money. Anecdotal reporting by law enforcement points to the use of MSBs in counterfeit check schemes and non-government charitable organizations (NGOs) utilizing MSBs to transfer proceeds internationally to support terrorist organizations and terrorist-related activities.

Several FBI field offices reported the laundering of millions of dollars derived from Internet extortion and fraud schemes through MSBs such as Western Union, PayPal, e-gold Limited, and other online payment systems.

Vulnerabilities particular to specific types of MSBs will be explored in the respective sub-chapters below.

### Geographic Concentration

Analysis of FinCEN data from October 1, 2002 through December 31, 2004 indicates that MSBs located in New York and California filed more MSB SAR forms than MSBs in any other state, followed by Arizona, Texas, Florida, Colorado, New Jersey, Massachusetts, Georgia, and Illinois. These numbers indicate a concentration of illicit financial activity in major, densely populated cities and along the Southwest border.

Law enforcement also identified geographic concentrations of MSB money laundering activity in highly-populated cities but did not identify California or the Southwest border as focal points for illicit MSB activity, despite the high volume of suspicious activity reported by MSBs in these regions to FinCEN.

With respect to destinations, most federal law enforcement agencies identified Mexico as the primary destination for suspicious funds sent through MSBs. Other prevalent destinations were Russia, Colombia, the Dominican Republic, and various locations in Central and South America. The majority of these investigations dealt with narcotics trafficking organizations. Investigations have also noted increased money laundering concerns among Middle Easterners in the United States operating MSBs and sending funds to Egypt, Sudan, and other locations in the Middle East.

### Regulation and Public Policy

As of December 31, 2001, all MSB principals (not individual agents) were required to register with FinCEN, listing the owner or controlling person. Each business that meets the definition of an MSB must register, except for the following:

- A business that is an MSB solely because it serves as an agent of another MSB;

- A business that is an MSB solely as an issuer, seller, or redeemer of stored value;

- The USPS and agencies of the United States, of any state, or of any political subdivision of any state; and

- A branch office of an MSB is not required to file its own registration form.

MSB registrations must be renewed every two years. Failure to register is punishable by a civil fine or criminal prosecution under 18 U.S.C. § 1960, which prohibits the operation of an unlicensed money transmitting business. For purposes of 18 U.S.C. § 1960, an unlicensed money transmitting business is a person who knowingly conducts, controls, manages, supervises, directs, or owns all or part of a money transmitting business, and who fails to register as required with FinCEN, or in

Table 3

MSB Suspicious Activity Reporting Ranking by States 10/1/02–12/31/04

| Ranking | State | % of MSB SARs Filed* | % of US MSB SARs |
|---------|-------|----------------------|-------------------|
| #1 | New York | 17% | |
| #1 | California | 17% | |
| #2 | Arizona | 9% | 49% |
| #3 | Texas | 8% | |
| #4 | Florida | 6% | |
| #5 | Colorado | 4% | |
| #6 | New Jersey | 4% | |
| #7 | Massachusetts | 3% | 25% |
| #8 | Georgia | 3% | |
| #9 | Illinois | 3% | |

*Percentages rounded to nearest whole number.

certain circumstances, operates without a required state license. MSBs which fail to register also may be liable for civil money penalties of up to $5,000 for each day the violation continues and a criminal penalty of up to five years imprisonment.

All MSBs must establish AML programs, and obtain and verify customer identity and record information about the transaction, including beneficiary information if received, for funds transfers of more than $3,000 regardless of whether the activity appears suspicious or not. They must also keep records regarding the cash purchase of money orders and traveler's checks between $3,000 and $10,000, and certain records regarding their currency exchange transactions. In addition, all MSBs are required to file reports of transaction in currency of more than $10,000.

As of January 1, 2002 most MSBs are required to report suspicious activity. The SAR requirement does not apply to check cashers or to sellers and redeemers of stored-value. An MSB is required to file a SAR on a transaction or series of transactions conducted or attempted by, at, or through the MSB if both of the following occur:

- The transaction or series of transactions involves or aggregates funds or other assets of $2,000 or more, and

- The MSB knows, suspects, or has reason to suspect that the transaction (or a pattern of transactions of which the transaction is a part) falls into one or more of the following categories:

  1. Involves funds derived from illegal activity or is intended or conducted in order to hide or disguise funds or assets derived from illegal activity as part of a plan to violate or evade any federal law or regulation or to avoid any transaction reporting requirement under federal law or regulation;

  2. Is designed to evade any BSA regulation;

  3. Has no business or apparent lawful purpose or is not the sort in which the particular customer would normally be expected to engage, and the MSB knows of no reasonable explanation

for the transaction after examining the available facts, including the background and possible purpose of the transaction; or

  4. Involves use of the MSB to facilitate criminal activity.

Despite the regulatory requirements, the majority of MSBs in the United States continue to operate without registering with FinCEN. Information obtained from SAR analysis indicates some lack of understanding by MSBs about registration requirements, especially among operators of small businesses that also provide MSB services. While some individuals made no attempt to register with FinCEN, others provided partial registration documentation. Other brokers, when given a thorough explanation of the registration process, were willing to comply with registration requirements. The relative novelty of the regulatory regime and the lack of familiarity by MSB operators about government and vice versa will continue to present challenges for both regulators and law enforcement.

IRS SB/SE has been delegated authority to examine MSBs for BSA compliance. A staff of several hundred IRS SB/SE full-time BSA examiners evaluates compliance with the reporting and record-keeping requirements of the BSA and Section 6050I of the Internal Revenue Code.

Monetary thresholds and the Sentencing Guidelines often impede the prosecution of 18 USC § 1960 violations. U.S. Attorney's Offices may be restricted by guidelines that force prosecutors to either decline or defer prosecutions of 18 USC § 1960 violations because the amount of money at issue is too small. Additionally, the relative newness of 18 USC § 1960 may limit its use by law enforcement and U.S. Attorney's Offices. Despite these factors, the Department of Justice has successfully prosecuted numerous 18 USC § 1960 violations, particularly in major metropolitan areas such as New York and Chicago.

The following sub-chapters will address the particular characteristics and vulnerabilities of Money Transmitters, Check Chasers, Currency Exchangers, Money Orders, and Stored Value Cards.

# MONEY TRANSMITTERS

The financial services industry, law enforcement, and regulators interchangeably refer to non-bank money transmitters as money remitters, wire remitters, and wire transmitters, hereinafter money transmitters.[36] The sheer volume and accessibility of money transmitters makes them attractive vehicles to money launderers operating in nearly every part of the world. Western Union runs the largest non-bank money transmitter network, with more than 225,000 agent locations in 195 countries and territories worldwide.[37]

As the overwhelming majority of wire transfers at MSBs are paid for with cash, money transmitters provide excellent camouflage for the initial introduction of the illicit proceeds into the financial system. Money transmitters offer inexpensive services, and often impose less rigorous AML programs and compliance than traditional financial institutions.

A funds transfer can generally be described as a series of steps, beginning with the originator's (customer's) instructions and including a payment message, which is used for the purpose of making payment to the beneficiary (receiving customer). There are a wide range of potential sources of funds for initiating a funds transfer, which include: cash, certified checks, cashier's checks, money orders, traveler's checks, account withdrawal, and credit and debit cards.

## Vulnerabilities

The vulnerabilities endemic to MSBs in general – discussed above – also apply to money transmitters. As with all industries subject to reporting thresholds, money launderers attempt to abuse money transmitters by structuring transactions below federal reporting thresholds. Owners or employees of registered money transmitters may help money launderers avoid reporting requirements by falsifying records to make it appear as though a large amount of laundered money was derived from a series of small transactions. Money transmitters may also knowingly permit individuals to make frequent structured transactions using false names and telephone numbers for each transaction.

The rapid movement of funds between accounts in different jurisdictions increases the complexity of investigations. In addition, investigations become even more difficult to pursue if the identity of the originator is not clearly shown in an electronic payment message.

Money transmitters remain a particularly attractive vehicle for money laundering due to several inherent characteristics of the industry:

- Large money transmitters maintain agent offices in thousands of cities and scores of countries, allowing customers to move funds from nearly any location directly to any other location;

- Money transmitters provide for rapid service, transmitting funds instantly or in days;

- The sheer volume of legitimate cash transactions provides an excellent camouflage for money laundering activity in the placement stage;[38]

- Money transmitter services are relatively inexpensive as compared with other means utilized by money launderers, often charging 10-20 percent per transmission; and

- Money transmitters increasingly provide online payment services and accept credit and debit cards. Although there are often identification safeguards in place – MSBs must verify identity with valid forms of identification and often utilize security features like password protection and online validation by third parties for signature verification – the lack of face-to-face interaction between the customer and the MSB limits the ability of MSBs to detect suspicious activity, as with other financial services provided through the Internet.

---

[36] Informal value transfer systems (IVTS), such as hawalas, are treated seperately in Chapter 4.

[37] *See* "About Western Union." Accessed at: http://www.westernunion.com/info/aboutUsIndex.asp?country=global.

[38] The three stages of money laundering are: (1) Placement, in which illicit proceeds are introduced into the financial system; (2) Layering, in which the criminal attempts to separate the proceeds from the crime through a series of transactions; and (3) Integration, in which the illicit proceeds are made to look legitimate through investment in legal assets.

Unregistered money transmitters offer money launderers many of the same advantages as registered money transmitters, with the added benefit of additional anonymity:

- The failure to follow federal reporting requirements reduces transparency yet further;

- Unregistered money transmitters frequently maintain coded records which may be inscrutable to investigators; and

- Unregistered transmitters may not advertise and may operate from locations with other primary purposes, such as gas stations, grocery stores, and residences, making them more difficult to detect. These businesses will often use such cash-intensive retail businesses to justify large-scale bank deposits and transfers.

## Demographic and Regional Concentrations

Ethnic immigrant communities are heavy users of money transmitter services, particularly to send money home to their native countries. Typically, members of these communities will use multiple services of an MSB, such as money transmission in conjunction with check cashing and/or currency exchange. DEA, ICE, FBI, FinCEN, and OCDETF have noted Middle Eastern, Asian, and Latin American – specifically Mexican – immigrant communities in major metropolitan areas as primary users of money transmitter services.

Frequently identified points of origin for money transmissions were New York, Los Angeles, Chicago, Dallas, Houston, Phoenix, Tucson, Seattle, and San Juan. Law enforcement reporting indicates that a large amount of illicit funds laundered through money transmission services are sent to the southwest border of the United

States. Roma, McAllen, Benita, Brownsville, Harlingen, Hidalgo, and Rio Grande City are the primary Texas border towns receiving wires, while Houston, and increasingly Dallas, are the primary cities receiving wires. The unusually large number of wires being received at the southwest border is particularly apparent in southern Arizona, where $12 are received for every $1 sent. As discussed below, this disparity may be accounted for in bulk cash movements south of the border. Some observed trends in predicate crimes by origin/destination are described in Table 4.

In the New York/New Jersey area, money transmittal businesses are extremely prevalent and witness a great deal of money laundering. Vulnerabilities particular to specific types of MSBs will be explored in the respective sub-chapters below. OCDETF identified the most prevalent area of suspicious activity as Jackson Heights, Queens, which purportedly contains the largest Colombian community outside of Colombia itself.

OCDETF also reports Colombian and Dominican drug trafficking organizations actively utilizing New England-based money transmitters to wire illicit drug proceeds to criminal recipients in Colombia and the Dominican Republic, despite some successful prosecutions in this arena.

Internationally, ICE notes that wires sent from the Los Angeles area were primarily destined for South/Central America, Asia, Europe, and the Middle East, while wires sent from the New York area were primarily destined for Colombia and the Dominican Republic.

## Money Transmitter Trends in Southern Arizona

Money transmissions received in southern Arizona and Texas are typically sent in amounts of less than $3,000.

Table 4

| Destination | Origin Points | Predominant Predicate Crime |
|---|---|---|
| Southern Arizona | California | Narcotics trafficking |
| Southwest Border | New York, New Jersey, North Carolina and Florida | Alien trafficking |
| Texas | New York, Florida, North Carolina, and New Jersey | Alien trafficking, narcotics trafficking to a lesser extent |

When alien trafficking is the predicate crime, it is believed that this amount does not indicate structuring but rather the relatively small amounts involved in individual instances of alien trafficking. When the transactions are received at the border, however, they become structured as the same receiver must collect the transactions individually in order to keep them under the $3,000 threshold.

From the southwest border, the funds are generally bulk shipped south. From Arizona, most of the money is smuggled across the border in passenger cars in amounts under $100,000, with a small amount retained

Table 5

| | Received in Arizona* | Originated in Arizona* |
|---|---|---|
| GA | 19.9 | 0.7 |
| IL | 25.7 | 0.7 |
| NC | 12.1 | 0.2 |
| NJ | 16.7 | 0.3 |
| NY | 31.6 | 1.1 |
| PA | 6.6 | 0.3 |
| **Total** | **112.6** | **3.4** |

*Millions of U.S. Dollars[1]

at the border to cover the operational costs of the alien smuggling operation. In Texas, 60-70 percent of the funds are bulk shipped across the border.[39]

After being bulk shipped across the border, the previously wired funds are generally returned to the United States. ICE reports that this is accomplished by wiring the money back to the United States, although various methods – some as simple as returning the funds via bulk cash shipment – can be used. When reentering the country, the illicit funds are documented, appear to be legitimate, and may then be used to meet the financial needs of the money launderers within the United States.

## Regulation and Public Policy

In addition to the rules applicable to all MSBs, money transmitters are required to collect information regarding wire transfers involving $3,000 or more and retain these records for five years. As of January 1, 2002, all money transmitters must maintain a list of agents and have it available for review. The list must include such information as the agent's name, depository institution, and the number of branches and subagents. A business acting solely as an agent of a money transmitter is not required to register with FinCEN. However, the agent must notify the money transmitter when it establishes subagents so that the transmitter may revise its agent list as required by FinCEN each January 1.

---

[39] Houston Money Laundering Initiative (HMLI).

# CHECK CASHERS

Check cashers provide essential services for persons without bank accounts. Criminals can and do abuse these services, however, to launder illicit funds, often in conjunction with money transmitters and informal value transfer systems (IVTS). Not all check cashers perform the same services and thus not all check cashers pose the same vulnerabilities or levels of risk.

## Vulnerabilities

Money launderers use check-cashing businesses to launder funds via third-party checking. To do this, a money launderer may make daily visits to small businesses in order to purchase checks made out to that business by uninvolved third parties. By selling these checks to the launderer, the business benefits by receiving immediate cash, avoiding banking or check cashing fees, avoiding income taxes, and passing on the risk of bad checks to the launderer. The launderer pays for the checks using illicit cash, and can then redeem the checks without causing the filing of a Currency Transaction Report (CTR) by not taking payment in cash. Money launderers sometimes purchase check cashing businesses outright, in which case checks can be deposited directly into the launderer's bank account, also without a CTR being filed.

Check-cashing businesses engaged in money laundering via third party checks typically will only withdraw a portion of the sum of checks being deposited, making up the remainder with dirty cash. This activity may generate a SAR. However, banks and law enforcement agencies may not immediately recognize this activity as suspicious, as the check-cashing business may reasonably hold accounts at other institutions from which the cash is being withdrawn. Illicit check-cashers may also arouse suspicion by withdrawing bills in large denominations.

To avoid scrutiny, money launderers will frequently send endorsed third-party checks out of the country to be cashed or deposited. When these checks are cashed or deposited at foreign banks, the U.S. bank may take note during the clearing process and file a SAR. Third-party checks are also used to send value overseas, akin to money orders. Because these checks are physically lighter and occupy less space than their cash equivalents, it is easier for money launderers to bulk ship or mail packages of these monetary instruments out of the country. For narcotics traffickers, shipping checks is also preferable to shipping currency because narcotics residues are less likely to adhere to paper checks than to currency, reducing the likelihood that police dogs will detect them.

Law enforcement has reported several examples of abuse in the check cashing industry. In one case, IRS-CI reported that numerous corporate checks stolen from the mail were eventually negotiated at a check casher. The FBI has witnessed an increase in money laundering through check cashing services and FBI field offices throughout the United States are observing large amounts of money flowing through structured deposits involving check cashing services. Drug trafficking organizations are noted as frequent users of this laundering method.

Others have observed these services used by undocumented immigrants sending money to Mexico and the Middle East. The lack of record-keeping requirements for check cashers hinders law enforcement efforts to identify the source of the suspect funds.

## Regulation and Public Policy

Check cashers, like most MSBs, must register with FinCEN. Although check cashers are required to file CTRs for cash transactions greater than $10,000, they are not currently required to file SARS (although they may do so voluntarily).

Only 24 states currently have specific check cashing legislation or regulations. Check cashers are often required to be licensed but are subject to less state regulatory oversight than other money service businesses, like sellers of money orders or traveler's checks. This is due, in part, to a perception that check cashing poses a comparatively smaller risk to consumers. Likewise, net worth requirements are typically less stringent for check cashers. State banking authorities or other supervisory bodies also examine these businesses less frequently.

The exemption of check cashers from SAR reporting requirements may hinder law enforcement efforts to identify laundering through this channel.

# CURRENCY EXCHANGERS

Currency exchangers, also referred to as currency dealers, money exchangers, *casas de cambio*, and bureaux de changes, provide conversion of bank notes of one country for that of another and may be abused by criminals in order to launder illicit funds, particularly during the placement stage of money laundering.

Although currency exchange, in and of itself, poses a less serious money laundering risk than the services provided by other MSBs, certain elements of the currency exchange sector, such as *casas de cambio*, play a major role in money laundering operations, particularly for narcotics organizations. Currency exchange is the MSB subject to the least state regulation, with fewer than ten states currently regulating this activity.

## Vulnerabilities

Currency exchange businesses are predominately located along shared borders, at international airports, and in large tourist areas. The services provided by currency exchange houses allow money launderers to exchange large quantities of small-denomination bills for large-denomination bills of the same or different currency. Thus exchanged, the bills can be more easily bulk shipped or deposited in bank accounts. Currency exchange houses are also used to provide additional cloaking in a funds transfer chain. An exchange house may, for example, accept cash from a customer which it then deposits in its own account at a commercial banking institution. The origin or source of the funds would be disguised because the bank will attribute ownership to the currency exchange business.

Currency exchange businesses also regularly offer money transmission services, compounding the threat by introducing the money transmitter risks discussed above.

### Casas de Cambio

*Casas de cambio* are currency exchange houses specializing in Latin American currencies and transactions. In the United States, these businesses are concentrated along the southwest border, with over 1,000 *casas de cambio* located along the border from California to Texas. These currency exchangers generally offer other MSB services, and often exist in combination with retail businesses such as gas stations and travel agencies. These businesses are generally unregistered and non-compliant with MSB SAR reporting requirements, and are suspected of being the primary non-bank money laundering mechanism in the southwest border area. Typical *casas de cambio* can launder as much as $5 million per month, primarily on behalf of drug traffickers. *Casas de cambio* are often run from mobile or temporary locations such as pickup trucks, trailers, sheds, and even telephone booths so that operations may be quickly relocated to avoid law enforcement. U.S.-based *casas de cambio* typically maintain close relationships with their Mexican counterparts in order to facilitate transactions such as funds transfers.

Some *casas de cambio* exist for the primary purpose of facilitating money laundering activities. Although *casas de cambio* are required to file Reports of International Transportation of Currency or Monetary Instruments (CMIRs) and Currency Transaction Reports (CTRs), they will commonly move money on behalf of many clients in a bulk transaction conducted under the name of the exchange house, thus cloaking the identity of the true originators. Any SARs filed in these cases by banks or other intermediaries will report the *casa de cambio* as the violator, often leading to an investigative dead end. Seized documents in raids conducted by the Venezuelan *Guardia Nacional* on *casas de cambio* and businesses in the Venezuelan state of Tachiria revealed that a number of *casas de cambio* were laundering drug proceeds originating from the United States through Venezuela to Colombia. Venezuela was being used to avoid Colombia's relatively high tariff on U.S. currency. It was later discovered that numerous *casas de cambio* involved in the money laundering process had U.S. dollar checking accounts through correspondent accounts held by major banks in Venezuela.

## Regulation and Public Policy

Currency exchangers are subject to general MSB regulations and are required to file SARs. In a sampling of 44 SARs filed by Currency Exchangers, FinCEN found that structuring was the most reported violation (29%), followed by altering the transaction to avoid reporting (20%), and two or more individuals conducting coordinated transactions (20%). The suspects reported in these SARs resided or transacted in Illinois and southwest border states, as well as Mexico, Canada,

Colombia, and Spain.

The amounts of violations reported in these SARs ranged from $0-$25 million. The violation ranges were as follows:

the filer, the suspect ceased doing business with this MSB; and

- Unusually large exchanges of currency. One SAR reported a suspect in connection with the exchange

Table 6

| Amount | Number of SARs | Percentage of Total Filings |
| --- | --- | --- |
| $0-$999 | 5 | 11% |
| $1,000-$9,999 | 31 | 70% |
| $10,000-$99,999 | 7 | 9% |
| $100,000-$25 million | 1 | -- |

With regard to the 13 SARs reporting violations involving money exchangers exclusively, the violation amounts ranged from $425 through $41,983, and structuring was the most reported violation, appearing in 7 of the 13 SARs (54%).

A review of money exchange SAR narratives reveals the following recurring patterns:

- The exchange of foreign currency for U.S. dollars (USD);

- Submitting U.S. currency in specific denominations such as $1's, $5's, and $10's;

- Odor on the currency;

- Two or more individuals working together to exchange pesos in an amount under the reporting requirement;

- Regular exchanges of similar amounts of currency. A California MSB reported a customer for regularly exchanging USD into pesos. Amounts ranging from $300-$800 USD were exchanged daily. The bills were all in small denominations under $1,000. At one point, the customer transacted over $1,000, prompting the exchange house to ask for ID and the purpose of the transactions. The suspect stated that she had a grocery store in California and bought supplies in Mexico. After she was questioned by

of 100,000 pesos for USD. The suspect balked when asked for ID, but did supply it. He later returned with a woman he identified as his client, who also exchanged 100,000 pesos for USD. A Texas MSB reported that, in one month, a Mexican suspect exchanged nearly $42,000. Another SAR reported a Spanish suspect who visited two Miami International Airport currency exchanger locations in three days and exchanged Euros for USD in the total amount of $21,290.

# MONEY ORDERS

Money orders are a highly versatile vehicle for money laundering, useful for a number of financial crimes ranging from smuggling narcotics trafficking proceeds to depositing illicit proceeds from alien smuggling and corporate fraud into bank accounts.

Money orders are used by approximately 30 million people annually to conduct business such as paying bills and sending money back to families in foreign countries. It is estimated that over 830 million money orders in excess of $100 billion are issued annually. The money order industry is small compared to that of other MSBs and easier to assess. Eighty percent of all money orders are issued by the USPS, Western Union, and Traveler's Express/MoneyGram. The remaining 20 percent are issued by smaller, regional companies scattered throughout the United States.

## Vulnerabilities

As a money laundering vehicle, money orders have several attractions. First, money orders can be issued in high-dollar denominations and are much less bulky than cash. Money orders are also replaceable if lost.

Anonymity is another major attraction. Money orders are issued anonymously for amounts under $3,000. Most money order sellers/issuers do not have any relationship with their customers and very little, if any, information is required to purchase a money order. Without originating information, it can be impossible for law enforcement to detect patterns of unlawful activity by an individual or group, or to track suspicious transactions to their source or ultimate recipient.

USPIS, FBI, DEA, and ICE investigations have all repeatedly noted dirty cash being converted to money orders to hide its true source and/or to shrink the physical size of the contraband in order to facilitate smuggling it out of the country. Commonly cited international destinations include Lebanon, the Palestinian territories, United Arab Emirates, Saudi Arabia, and Central and South America.

Financial hubs that see the greatest volume of money order activity are New York/New Jersey, Los Angeles, El Paso, Dallas, Miami, Boston, and San Francisco. DEA, USPIS, ICE, and the New York/New Jersey High Risk Money Laundering and Related Financial Crimes Areas (HIFCA) [40] all report significant money laundering activity with money orders in these regions. OCDETF has consistently reported that approximately 20 percent of its newly-initiated money laundering investigations contains a money order component. Law enforcement, primarily ICE and DEA, and the regulatory community have seen a steady stream of money order use by launderers moving bulk cash from narcotics transactions to Mexico and other regions of Latin America. DEA and ICE report an area of increasing concern is the use of Mexican *casas de cambio* used to transport proceeds through money orders into Mexico. The vulnerabilities presented by money orders and the relative lack of regulatory oversight of *casas de cambio* in many foreign countries create an attractive environment for individuals seeking to launder illicit proceeds.

---

[40] HIFCAs were conceived in the Money Laundering and Financial Crimes Strategy Act of 1998 as a means of concentrating law enforcement efforts at the federal, state, and local levels in high intensity money laundering zones. HIFCAs may be defined geographically or they can also be created to address money laundering in an industry sector, a financial institution, or group of financial institutions.

*The illustration below presents a typical cycle of money laundering through the use of money orders.[41]*

money orders. The great majority of these money order-related SARs (93%) were filed by USPS. USPS reported approximately $296.9 million in suspicious money order activity equaling approximately .01% of the total face value issued in 2003. In 2004, USPS reported $408.5 million in suspicious money order activity, equaling approximately .014% of the total face value issued. The increase from 2003 to 2004 by .005% is believed to reflect USPS's lowering of its "back-end" threshold for detecting suspicious activity from $10,000 to $5,000.

Trends identified in the SARs filed include the following:

- The purchase of multiple, structured money orders on the same day or within a short period of time; on many SARs it was noted that when the customers were informed of the reporting threshold, they changed their purchase to lower amounts;

- Money order deposits to the same bank account composed of multiple, sequentially numbered money orders;

- Customers lacking proper identification, or providing false identification, leading some filers to conclude that these customers could be illegal aliens;

- Structured purchases frequently followed by the deposit of the money orders into the same bank account;

## Regulation and Public Policy

Regulatory requirements for MSBs that issue money orders are the same as those for MSBs in general, as set out above. In addition, many money order businesses impose their own lower dollar thresholds, such as not selling more than $2,000 in money orders to a customer in a given day, which obviate the need for CTR reporting.

Of the total SARs filed for MSBs from October 1, 2002 through December 31, 2004, 32 percent involved

- Individuals coming into the Post Office together, but separating inside to make the purchases from different tellers because the combined total of the money orders purchased exceeded the reporting threshold; and

- Money order purchases being paid for with currency in specific denominations, sometimes bundled into stacks, indicating organized-crime involvement.

Anti-money laundering training is required of money order businesses, but this training can be quite cursory. Common vendors of money orders, such as small convenience stores, may neither understand nor value BSA compliance. When AML training is offered, it is typically thin, such as requiring employees to read a brief pamphlet. The fact that the workforce at these businesses is frequently comprised of part-time, younger, and less-educated employees with an extraordinarily high turnover rate, further complicates the training effort.

There is also an accountability gap. All money order issuers, aside from the USPS, rely to a large extent on licensed agents, rather than employees, to sell their instruments. The parent firms have a responsibility to review activity across their agent network but are not required to review individual SARs. Indeed, some firms specifically discourage their agents from submitting SARs to the parent firm.[42]

Western Union and MoneyGram combined – which represent over 50% of the money orders issued in the United States – represented only 1 percent of all SARs filed from October 1, 2002 through December 31, 2004, where money laundering was listed as the Category of Violation and where money orders was identified as the Financial Service(s) Involved. By comparison, USPS – which represents one-quarter of all money orders issued in the United States – represented 93 percent of such SAR activity.

---

[42] *See, e.g.,* Travelers Express "Anti-Money Laundering Compliance Guide," July 2002. Accessed at: http://www.moneygram.com/forms/agentguide.pdf.

# STORED VALUE CARDS

Stored value cards (sometimes referred to as prepaid cards) are an emerging cash alternative for both legitimate consumers and money launderers alike. The term "stored value cards" can cover a variety of uses and technologies. Some cards have embedded data processing chips, some have a magnetic stripe, and some cards (e.g. prepaid phone service cards) just have an access number or password printed on them (the card itself cannot access or transfer cash).

Stored value cards can be characterized as operating within either an "open" or "closed" system (See Table 7). Open system cards can be used to connect to global debit and automated teller machine (ATM) networks. The cards can be used for purchases at any merchant or to access cash at any ATM that connects to the global payment networks.[43] Such open system card programs generally do not require a bank account or face-to-face verification of cardholder identity. Funds can be prepaid by one person, with someone else in another country accessing the cash via ATM. Open system stored value cards typically may be reloaded, allowing the cardholder to add value.

Closed system[44] cards are limited in that they can only be used to buy goods or services from the merchant issuing the card or a select group of merchants or service providers that participate in a network that is limited geographically or otherwise. Examples of closed system cards include retail gift cards, mall cards, and mass transit

system cards, as well as the multipurpose cards used on overseas U.S. military bases and on college campuses. These cards may be limited to the initial value posted to the card or may allow the card holder to add value.[45]

Stored value cards offer individuals without bank accounts an alternative to cash and money orders. Target markets include teenagers, the unbanked, adults unable to qualify for a credit card, and immigrants sending cash to family outside the country. The unbanked in the United States comprise an estimated 10 million households and 75 million individuals.[46] A growing segment of the stored value card market consists of businesses and government agencies using plastic cards to replace paper vouchers, checks, and cash for per diems, insurance and health benefit payments, and even payroll. Issuers see the greatest fee potential, however, among the unbanked, who, by using the cards in place of cash and money orders, generate transaction fees with every purchase and every cash withdrawal.[47]

## Vulnerabilities

Stored value cards provide a compact, easily transportable, and potentially anonymous way to store and access cash value. Open system cards lower the barrier to the U.S. payment system, allowing individuals without a bank account to access illicit cash via ATMs globally. Closed system cards, primarily store gift cards, present more limited opportunities and a correspondingly lower risk as a means to move monetary value out of the country. Yet federal law enforcement agencies

---

[43] International networks on which open system cards can be used include Visa's Plus (ATM) and Interlink (point-of-sale) networks and MasterCard's Cirrus (ATM) and Maestro (point-of-sale) networks.

[44] Smart cards are another version of a closed system card, but are not widely used in the U.S. In some countries, smart cards have an embedded data processing chip that carries bank-issued electronic money. The cards can transfer money directly to participating merchants without the transaction going through an intermediary. The merchant or service provider's bank redeems the stored electronic payments as conventional cash from the bank that issued the e-money. In some countries, smart cards have achieved modest acceptance for domestic small-value purchases. Smart cards are also used in countries with inefficient telecommunications, so that merchants do not need to query a central database for transaction authorizations.

[45] Some retailers do offer redemption of gift cards for cash, but they do not openly advertise that this is an option. In this scenario, the gift cards can be used to launder funds and hide the paper trail of not only the source of the funds used to purchase the cards, but also where the funds go if the cards are redeemed for cash.

[46] Hillebrand, Gail, Payment Mechanism: New Products, New Problems, Consumers Union, presentation delivered at the Federal Reserve Bank of Chicago, May 29, 2003. Accessed at: http://www.chicagofed.org/news_and_conferences/conferences_and_events/files/2003_payments_conference_gail_hillebrand_presentation.pdf.

[47] Issuers have triggered a backlash by going beyond transaction fees, adding charges for checking a balance, adding cash, or even doing nothing ("inactivity" fees), drawing criticism from consumer rights advocates and attorneys general. For example, California, Washington, and New Hampshire have passed laws curtailing prepaid card fees and practices. Connecticut, Massachusetts, New Hampshire, and New York have filed lawsuits against the Visa-branded Simon Malls card specifically because of fees.

have reported both categories of stored value cards are used as alternatives to smuggling physical cash.

Stored value card programs often accept applications online, via fax, or through local check cashing outlets, convenience stores, and other retailers. Programs that lack customer identification procedures and systems to monitor transactions for suspicious activity present significant money laundering vulnerabilities, particularly if there are liberal limits or no limits on the amount of cash that can be prepaid into the card account or accessed through ATMs. Offshore banks also offer stored value cards with cash access through ATMs internationally. Further, programs designed to facilitate cross-border remittance payments often allow multiple cards to be issued per account so that friends and family in the receiving country can use the cards to access cash and make purchases. These programs can also be used to launder money if effective AML policies, procedures, and controls are not in place.

Law enforcement agents on the El Dorado Task Force[48] in New York found they could use false identification to obtain prepaid cards and even have the cards sent to a U.S. Post Office box. Secret Service investigations have found that not only do some prepaid card applicants use false identification; they fund their initial deposits with stolen credit cards and money from other illicit sources.

DEA, ICE, and IRS-CI have all found prepaid cards used in conjunction with bulk cash smuggling. Drug dealers load cash onto prepaid cards and send the cards to their drug suppliers outside the country. The suppliers then use the cards to withdraw money from a local ATM.[49]

Phone cards and other "closed" system prepaid cards also present opportunities for money laundering. The cards can be purchased for cash and transferred from one person to another domestically or internationally and eventually resold. Closed system cards are not currently subject to CMIR reporting when moved across U.S. borders.[50] ICE sees the potential for a variation on the Black Market Peso Exchange (BMPE)[51] with phone cards exchanged for drug money. Also, prepaid cards for wireless and long-distance service are a cash-intensive business, offering an opportunity to integrate dirty money. Distributors of prepaid phone cards can generate more than $100 million in cash annually.

## Regulation and Public Policy

A stored value card used in an ATM to access cash from a prepaid account operates the same way as a debit card accessing a bank account via ATM, but there can be a substantial difference in how the two cards are issued and the accounts managed. Banks and other depository financial institutions are obligated to have a customer identification program (CIP) and to report large or suspicious transactions (SARs). "Issuers, sellers, and redeemers of stored value" are classed as an MSB under the relevant regulations[52] and are required to have an AML program but are not required to file SARs[53] or to register with FinCEN.[54]

Although open system stored value cards use the same payment networks as some bank-issued debit cards (e.g. Visa's Plus and Interlink, and MasterCard's Cirrus and Maestro), stored value cardholders generally are not

---

[48] Created in 1992 to target money laundering in New York, the El Dorado Task Force became one of the nation's most successful money laundering task forces. It is led by ICE and includes representatives from 29 federal, state, and local agencies.

[49] Even prepaid cards for long distance and wireless services are proving to be money laundering tools as the wholesale distribution system for these cards is cash-intensive, offering cover for money laundering.

[50] A Report of International Transportation of Currency or Monetary Instruments (CMIR) must be filed by each person who physically transports, mails, or ships, or causes to be physically transported, mailed, or shipped currency or other monetary instruments in an aggregate amount exceeding $10,000 at one time from the United States to any place outside the United States or into the United States from any place outside the United States (FinCEN Form 105).

[51] The BMPE involves drug suppliers in Colombia working with a currency broker. Rather than bringing their illicit dollars from the U.S. back to Colombia, the drug suppliers turn the cash over to a currency broker who can provide pesos in Colombia. The broker keeps the dollars in the U.S., selling them to Colombian importers who need the foreign currency to purchase goods from U.S. suppliers. The importers pay for the foreign currency with the pesos in Colombia that ultimately go to the drug suppliers.

[52] See 31 CFR. §103.11(uu)(3) and (4).

[53] See 31 CFR. §§103.120 and 103.20(a)(5).

[54] See 31 CFR §103.41(a)(1).

obligated to have a bank account. A common model for stored value card programs is for a firm independent of the bank to process all cardholder transactions through a "pooled" bank account held in the name of the firm managing the card program. In this arrangement, the bank may have no direct contact with the individual cardholders. Under current regulations, when a stored value card firm uses a "pooled" account maintained in its name for cardholder transactions, banks are required only to conduct customer due diligence and customer identification procedures on the card management firm and not the individual cardholders.[55]

MasterCard International and Visa USA have suggested AML guidelines for card issuers including account limits and requirements to verify identification. But web sites for stored value card programs that promote cardholder anonymity and flaunt a lack of AML policies suggest that this guidance may not be consistently enforced. Finally, a byproduct of the global market for and use of stored value products is that domestic action alone will not adequately address the vulnerability presented by these products. Issuers outside of the United States generally are not subject to the BSA,[56] yet the cards they issue may be used in the United States.

---

[55]   *See* Deposit Insurance Coverage; Stored Value Cards and Other Nontraditional Access Mechanisms, Notice Of Proposed Rulemaking Federal Register 70:151 (8 August 2005): 455710-45581.

[56]   Bank Secrecy Act, Titles I and II of Pub. L. 91-508, as amended, codified at 12 U.S.C. § 1829b, 12 U.S.C. §§ 1951-1959, and 31 U.S.C. §§ 5311-5332.

Table 7

| Card Programs | Characteristics | Target Market | Possible Issuer Benefit | Potential Threat | Examples |
|---|---|---|---|---|---|
| Gift cards and prepaid phone services (Single service provider) | Store- or brand-specific (No payment network branding) Cards often sold in pre-set denominations/Merchant collects full value up-front | High frequency customers | Float[57], increased sales | BMPE-style ML[58]: exchanging cash for cards/Use as alternative currency/Distribution method is cash intensive creating ML threat | Retailer-specific and Phone service cards |
| Gift cards: Multiple Merchants | Multi-merchant gift card: can be used for purchases only (no ATM)/Can be payment network branded | Gift givers | Float, sales, and transaction fees[59] | Money laundering through bulk card acquisition and resale | Mall card |
| Payroll cards | Creates account to facilitate direct deposit/ Cards can be used at ATM & POS[60] | Unbanked workers who are being paid by cash or check | Fee income (lower cost to employer) | Fraudulent businesses could use to pay terrorists or launder money | Various |
| Remittance cards | Cards are issued for friends & family to use at cross-border ATM & POS | Individuals who send cross-border remittances | Fee income | Provides anonymous cross-border access to funds for purchases or cash | Various |
| General use cash cards | Debit card good at ATM & POS to access pre-funded account | Unbanked, teens, & those unable to qualify for credit card | Fee income | Provides anonymous cross-border access to funds for purchases or cash | Various |
| Function-specific cards | Replaces paper money, tickets, and forms for a variety of functions | Businesses & government agencies processing high volume of cash, checks or vouchers | Lower cost processing | None apparent | Transit systems/ Health savings accounts/ Govt. benefit programs |

---

[57] Merchant earns interest on idle card funds.
[58] Black Market Peso Exchange-type money laundering.
[59] Purchases with bank cards generate transaction fees for the issuing bank.
[60] Point-of-sale.

## Chapter 3
# ONLINE PAYMENT SYSTEMS

New and innovative online payment services are emerging globally in response to market demand from individuals and online merchants. Individuals, some of whom may not have a bank account or are unable to qualify for a credit card, are looking to online payment services to enable online shopping, electronic bill payment, and person-to-person funds transfers. And some online merchants are demonstrating a willingness to accept new electronic methods of payment that are less expensive than credit cards. These payment services function as online payment systems, accepting funds in a variety of ways for the purpose of transferring payment either to a merchant or an individual.

Individuals wanting to shop online or participate in an online auction can use an existing bank account, credit card, wire transfer, money order, and even cash to fund an account with an online intermediary that will facilitate the payment. Some online payment services exist to facilitate transactions for online gambling and adult content sites that U.S.-based money transmitters typically will not service.[61] U.S. citizens can access payment services online that are based outside of the United States and transfer funds either electronically or by mail.

Online merchants, particularly those in sectors with high "chargeback" rates, are generating demand for new payment methods.[62] These markets embrace online payment systems that set their own clearing and settlement terms absent any consumer protection or financial regulation. Typically, transactions through these service providers are considered final with no recourse for individuals who believe they have been defrauded. The consequence, according to federal law enforcement agencies, is that these systems have become favorite payment mechanisms for online perpetrators of fraudulent investment schemes and other illegal activity.

Some online payment services defy conventional business models. "Digital currency" dealers, for example, use precious metals (gold, palladium, platinum, and silver) as the store of value for online transactions and split the transaction process between two business entities: the digital currency exchange service and the digital currency dealer. Despite the appropriation of the term "digital currency" to describe the use of precious metals for online payments, digital currency remains one of many common phrases with "digital," or "cyber" or "e–," used to refer to any electronic payment initiated online.[63]

The systems work as follows: A person wanting to use gold for an online purchase would first open a gold account with a digital currency dealer and then fund the account through an exchange service. Each exchange service sets its own terms, so that while some may only accept transfers from bank or credit card accounts, others will accept cash and money orders.[64] Similarly, each exchange service offers different options for receiving funds. The result is that some service providers pose a greater risk for money laundering.

The oldest and best known of the digital currency services is e-gold Ltd., licensed in Nevis, with almost 2

---

[61] In 2002, PayPal, perhaps the largest and best-known online payment system (339.9 million payments worth $18.9 billion in 2004), stopped providing payment services for online gambling and adult content sites. PayPal, was launched in 1998, and today has 63 million member accounts in 45 countries. In addition to facilitating transactions for sites PayPal no longer services, emerging online payment systems also are targeting countries in which PayPal does not operate. PayPal is a division of e-Bay, a publicly-held, U.S.-based corporation, and is licensed in the jurisdictions where it permits customers to send and/or receive money. (*Source*: http://www.paypal.com) PayPal has also registered with FinCEN as an MSB.

[62] When a customer using a credit card disputes a charge, the customer is said to "charge back" the transaction. Managing charge backs is costly to merchants who can be fined by their bank for frequent disputes or required to pay higher transaction fees. Online gambling and adult content web sites are among industries prone to chargebacks and are charged higher credit card fees than brick and mortar businesses.

[63] The use of the term "currency" in this context is not strictly correct. Currency is something monetized by a monetizing authority, generally central banks. Rather than being used as currency, these precious metals are used as a part of a barter exchange (one party agrees to exchange a quantity of gold for various goods or services).

[64] In addition to other funding options, a California-based digital currency exchanger accepts cash delivered by courier. Another service provider based in Panama also accepts cash, but advises: "We have a limit of $2,500.99 per day, per bank for cash deposits. For bigger amounts please send wires or postal money orders."

million accounts.[65]    E-gold indicates on its web site that its metal holdings provide a form of guarantee that should convey trustworthiness[66] – a feature often lacking among unregulated online payment services. Digital currency dealers also promote the global acceptance of precious metals, observing that a buyer paying with gold need not worry about access to or acceptance of underlying currencies. Merchants, online service providers, and individuals who are willing to receive payment in precious metals are allocated a quantity based on the day's market price. While taking delivery of the actual metal is an option, recipients can also sell the metal through a digital currency "exchanger" and receive payment in a more conventional form.

The Global Digital Currency Association (GDCA) is a trade association of digital currency dealers and exchangers pressing for self-regulation. The GDCA provides a public ranking of its membership and offers arbitration procedures.[67]  However, the GDCA constitution makes no mention of AML policies and procedures or of adhering to international AML recommendations such as those promulgated by the Financial Action Task Force (FATF).[68]  The GDCA manages member conduct through its "reputation ranking system," which allocates or subtracts points based on length of membership and dispute and dispute record. (See Figure 1)

## Vulnerabilities

Online payment services function as international person-to-person payment systems.  By crossing jurisdictional lines these services potentially create difficulties for authorities pursuing enforcement or legal actions. Although individuals may use credit cards, wire transfers, or other bank payment tools to move funds to online payment systems, the investigative trail for law enforcement ends there when service providers do not have effective customer identification or recordkeeping practices.  In addition, the trail is further shortened when service providers accept cash and money orders to fund accounts.

U.S. federal law enforcement agencies have found that some online payment services are ill-equipped to verify customer identification[69] and some openly promote anonymous payments.  The type of personal information required for opening an account with a digital currency dealer or exchanger or online payment system varies by service provider.

The FBI reports six individuals indicted in a Ponzi scheme in March 2004 used a digital currency exchange service to transfer some $50 million from 26,000 investors.  The FBI Crime Complaint Center has received a number of complaints regarding Internet auction fraud, investment schemes, and computer intrusions all involving digital currency services.

U.S. federal law enforcement agencies currently are investigating a credit and debit card fraud ring that uses stolen account information to make unauthor-

Figure 1

---

**GDCA Membership Ranking Key**
(excerpted from the GDCA Constitution)*

**Membership Awards:**

- Silver – Awarded to members known to be reputable and trustworthy

- Gold – Awarded to members known to be trustworthy, without any reported or reputed valid customer complaints over a one year period

- Platinum – Rarely awarded, and when, then only to outstanding members who are well known, have shown to be beyond reproach and who head outstandingly upright operations, pillars of the industry

- Palladium – Awarded to long-serving Committee members and officers of the GDCA who qualify for Platinum awards.

Points may be earned or lost [at the discretion of the GDCA].

* Accessed at: http://www.gdcaonline.org.

---

[65] E-Dinar is a spin-off of e-gold, and is affiliated with the Islamic Mint, a private organization dedicated to reviving the gold and silver currencies described in the Koran, the gold dinar and silver dirham. The target market for the e-Dinar is the more than one billion Muslims directed by the Koran to pay "zakat" or 2.5% of one's net worth annually to be distributed to the needy and the poor. Accessed at: http://www.e-dinar.com.

[66] Accessed at: http://www.e-gold.com.

[67] Accessed at: http://www.gdcaonline.org/.

[68] FATF Standards. Accessed at: http://www.fatf-gafi.org/pages/0,2966,en_32250379_32236920_1_1_1_1_1,00.html.

[69] Money services businesses are not required under the BSA to have customer identification programs. They are required to have programs in place to perform necessary customer due diligence appropriate to the risks presented, and to comply with all recordkeeping and reporting requirements under the BSA.

ized withdrawals. The illicit funds are then laundered through digital currency accounts and through open system prepaid cards. Funds transferred to digital currency accounts can be sent via money transmitters globally. Similarly, funds transferred to prepaid card accounts can be accessed via ATMs globally.

## Regulation and Public Policy

In the United States, money transmitters are among MSBs required to register with FinCEN,[70] are subject to AML reporting and recordkeeping requirements,[71] and are often required to be licensed on the state level. Whether an online payment system or digital currency service meets the definition of a money transmitter pursuant to BSA regulations, though, depends upon its location and the ways in which it participates in or conducts transactions.[72] Many online payment systems are based outside the United States and are not subject to U.S. jurisdiction. Some online payment systems may be licensed in one country and maintain operations (including staff, computer systems, and customers) in various other countries without a physical retail presence anywhere. Determining which legal entity has jurisdiction for regulatory and enforcement purposes can be challenging.[73] Potential users around the world now are finding they can go online to access payment options that may be unavailable from a domestically-regulated service provider.

Unregulated online payment systems do not have consistent or reliable AML policies and procedures. Opportunities for domestic regulation and enforcement are limited by jurisdictional issues. Without international coordination to encourage unregulated online payment

systems to adopt and adhere to FATF AML policies and procedures, any single jurisdiction acting alone may have only limited success in this regard.

---

[70] 31 CFR § 103.41.

[71] 31 CFR §§ 103.125 and 103.20.

[72] 31 CFR § 103.11(uu) states: "*Money services business.* Each agent, agency, branch, or office within the United States of any person doing business, whether or not on a regular basis or as an organized business concern, in one or more of the capacities listed in paragraphs (uu)(1) through (uu)(6) of this section." 31 CFR § 103.11(uu) (5) states: "Money transmitter--(i) In general. *Money transmitter*: (A) Any person, whether or not licensed or required to be licensed, who engages as a business in accepting currency, or funds denominated in currency, and transmits the currency or funds, or the value of the currency or funds, by any means through a financial agency or institution, a Federal Reserve Bank or other facility of one or more Federal Reserve Banks, the Board of Governors of the Federal Reserve System, or both, or an electronic funds transfer network; or (B) Any other person engaged as a business in the transfer of funds."

[73] Most jurisdictions, including the U.S., have not established a licensing or regulatory framework for online payment systems with no physical presence in the jurisdiction. An exception is the U.K. where online payment systems come under the umbrella term "electronic money issuers" and are subject to the Financial Services and Markets Act 2000. *See* Financial Services Authority, *The Regulation of Electronic Money Issuers.* Accessed at: http://www.fsa.gov.uk/pubs/cp/cp117.pdf.

## Chapter 4
# INFORMAL VALUE TRANSFER SYSTEMS

Informal Value Transfer Systems (IVTS)[74] are efficient remittance systems based on trust that operate primarily within ethnic communities. IVTS include various centuries-old remittance systems centered in ethnic/national communities, the most utilized of which are Hawala/Hundi (South Asia),[75] Fei ch'ien (China), Phoe Kuan (Thailand), and Door to Door (Philippines). Although these systems primarily service legitimate customers and purposes, criminal elements exploit IVTS to launder/transfer proceeds because of their lack of transparency and low costs. Indeed, these systems have historically proven themselves to be among the safest methods to transfer money without visibility. IVTS provide transfers to and from areas where modern financial services are unavailable, inaccessible, unaffordable, or localities where corruption within the financial system is prevalent. The system provides rapid funds transfers (usually within hours of the transaction's initiation), under a safeguard of trust and reliability.

IVTS can be operated from virtually any location with access to a communication network such as e-mail, fax, or telephone. IVTS has been observed in convenience stores and gas stations, souvenir shops, ethnic barber shops, and restaurants, as well as private residences.

The following fact pattern lays out a typical IVTS transaction:

> In country A, a client hands over a sum of money to an IVTS broker and requests that the equivalent amount (usually in the currency of the receiving country) be sent to a designated recipient in country B. The sending broker relays all the necessary information concerning the transaction to a counterpart broker in country B either through telephone, facsimile, or email. At this stage of the process, a "collection code" is agreed upon between the two brokers. The broker in country A will then communicate this code to the client, who, in turn, will relay it to the designated recipient in country B. The broker in country B will give the money to the recipient upon presentation of the collection code. If the sending client is also the recipient, he would have to present the code to the counterpart broker, upon arriving in country B before the money could be released to him. In many cases, the payment will be made by the counterpart broker to the designated recipient within hours after the request to remit money was placed by the client in country A. The income of the broker from the transaction may come from charging a commission ranging from 0.25% to 1.25% of the amount involved or from disparities in currency exchange rates.

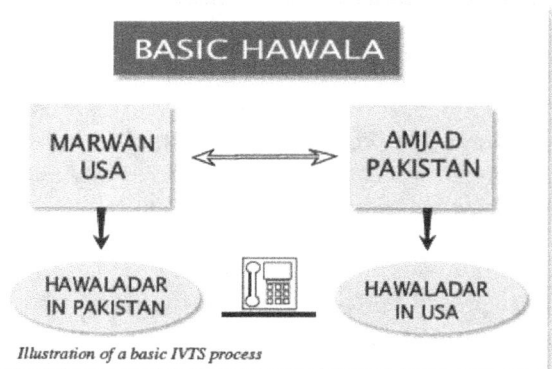

Illustration of a basic IVTS process

It is virtually impossible to ascertain the full extent of IVTS activity in the United States due to the opacity of the sector and the absence of registration by most IVTS

---

[74] IVTS are often referred to as Alternative Remittance Systems (ARS) in the international sector. ARS are operated by entities (alternative remittance operators) for moving money or other forms of stored value between countries on behalf of customers who do not wish to directly use the "formal" banking system. *See* Asia Pacific Group-Alternative Remittance Regulation Implementation Package (July 2003).

[75] Although listed separately, in many countries users of hawala and hundi often use the terms interchangeably to describe the hawala transfer process. Hawala, meaning transfer in Arabic, is a remittance vehicle. Hundi, meaning collect, began centuries ago as a form of IOU, bill of exchange, and remittance vehicle. Currently, various countries misuse the term hundi to describe the hawala transfer process.

operators. SAR information and law enforcement observations offer some clues, however, to the functioning of this sector.

### Bank Secrecy Act Data

SAR data currently provide the best means of identifying IVTS trends. A review of SAR activity for the period March 2003-October 2004 identified 174 SARs indicating IVTS activity. The primary geographic locations in which IVTS appeared are Texas (14.4%), Illinois (12.1%), Minnesota (6.32%), Arizona (5.75%), Georgia (5.75%), and Michigan (5.75%). The subjects of these violations were identified as operating cash-intensive businesses for the purpose of commingling proceeds from the IVTS with their legitimate business earnings. Typical businesses associated with suspicious IVTS activity included gas/convenience markets, restaurants/lounges/liquor stores, video stores, and clothing or jewelry stores.

Suspicious transactions indicating IVTS activity included the following techniques:

- Multiple deposits of combinations of cash, money orders, or third-party checks;

- Multiple deposits of combinations of cash, money orders, or third-party checks made to the same account from different states;

- Daily deposits;

- Multiple structured deposits; and,

- Multiple incoming wire transfers followed by any of the activities listed below:

    1. Outgoing wire transfers, either domestic or international;

    2. Outgoing transfers via Automated Clearing House debits to known MSBs;

    3. Checks written to cash by the accountholder;

    4. Checks written to or endorsed by known MSBs; or

    5. ATM cash withdrawals in remote locations, including other countries.

Additional indicators useful for law enforcement in identifying an IVTS operation include:

- Structured deposits followed by wire transfers to unrelated businesses in Southeast/Southwest Asia;

- Multiple financial ledgers (one for legitimate transfers, one for criminal activity, possibly an additional ledger for settling accounts between brokers);

- A high volume of mail and packages from out of state that contain various monetary instruments such as checks or money orders;

- Short telephone calls coming into the broker (instructions from the customer sending funds);

- Numerous lengthy telephone calls made to overseas recipients (indicates the broker is coordinating with counterparts and placing orders); and

- Fax transmittal logs. Faxes sent may be a roll-up of the day's transactions or may be single transactions. Faxes may contain the name of a sender (not necessarily a real name), beneficiary, or code used by the receiving broker to identify the beneficiary.

### Law Enforcement Data

Law enforcement agencies encountered common patterns in their IVTS investigations, reporting concentrations of IVTS activity among Middle Eastern communities, as well as Somali, Yemeni, Pakistani, Afghani, Filipino, Indonesian, Chinese, African, Indian, and Latino communities. Transfers by these communities are primarily directed at areas with non-existent, unaffordable, or untrustworthy financial institutions. Consistent with the BSA data, law enforcement agencies observed IVTS operations utilizing cash-intensive businesses (e.g., convenience stores/gas stations) to commingle funds.

In addition to the inherent difficulties in penetrating IVTS networks and proving the elements of an 18 U.S.C. § 1960 case, law enforcement has faced difficulties due to the relative novelty of the statute and monetary threshold issues imposed by the United States Attorney Offices. Despite these factors, law enforcement has had some increasing success in prosecuting unlicensed and criminal IVTS operators. Since the enactment of § 1960, ICE has initiated more than 260 IVTS investigations and executed more than 100 search warrants in connection with these cases. During this period, ICE investigations into unlicensed MSBs have resulted in roughly 120 arrests, 130 indictments, and the seizure of some $23 million.

A former Customs Service case illustrates the difficulties in building IVTS cases. (See Case Example 2)

---

### CASE EXAMPLE 2

**Law Enforcement Challenges**

Bank records seized pursuant to search warrants revealed that the subject, using a personal account and his business (a convenience store) account, sent checks totaling approximately $300,000 to various individuals in Yemen during the years 1998 - 2002. Cash deposits were made simultaneous to the writing of the checks, and slightly exceeded the amounts of the checks (indicative of a fee being charged). The checks sent were subsequently negotiated at various banks in Yemen. The tracking of the flow of funds stopped there.

The subject, during his interview, stated he knew what a hawala was and the types of fees associated with its operation. However, he insisted that he was not operating one, and that he was simply sending money to support family members in his native Yemen. No lists or records of clients were ever uncovered; investigators were unable to corroborate any testimony because the primary witnesses were in Yemen; and no one in the local Yemeni community was able to state that the subject and/or others were operating hawalas. Because of the lack of corroboration, the 18 USC § 1960 part of the case was discontinued and the subject was indicted on other charges.

*This investigation was initiated as a result of the former Customs Service's Operation Green Quest.*

---

## Vulnerabilities

IVTS offer several business advantages over formal remitters[76] such as Western Union and MoneyGram, including the following:

- A formal remitter will charge the sender approximately 10-20% of the total amount transferred whereas an IVTS will typically charge 0.25%-1.5%, if any commission at all;

- Formal remitters provide service to larger population centers while IVTS provide service to the same, as well as remote areas of the world;

- Transfers initiated by formal remittance agencies typically take days or weeks, whereas IVTS transactions are conducted within hours with at-home pick-up and delivery services; and

- Recipients must present identification when receiving transfers at a formal agency, whereas IVTS only require an anonymous code for receipt of funds.

All of these factors make IVTS attractive to lawful individuals as well as money launderers.[77] In addition, money launderers are drawn to IVTS for the unparalleled confidentiality that they offer, allowing them to conduct transactions in near anonymity. IVTS records are typically spotty and omit all but the most perfunctory customer identification information. Ledgers may be kept in foreign languages or in initials and codes and are difficult to decipher without cooperation of the remitter. Records may also be destroyed within a short period of time after their creation.

Even where records exist and are comprehensible, IVTS transactions may be routed through third party accounts of individuals or companies. Law enforcement investigations of IVTS have encountered nominee accounts, sometimes referred to as "benami,"[78] which effectively

---

[76] IVTS are informal remittance systems, as they exist and operate outside of (or parallel to) conventional regulated banking and financial channels; often referred to as the formal financial sector.

[77] *See also* FinCEN Advisory Issue 33. Acccessed at: http://www.fincen.gov/advis33.pdf.

[78] *"Benami"* or nominee accounts are culturally accepted in ethnic groups that also engage in hawala. Because the true beneficiary of a transaction is not the person under whose name the transaction takes place, it is very hard to identify the owners of criminal proceeds and people who engage in illegal activities.

stop the money trail. Law enforcement agents are also faced with language and cultural barriers when trying to communicate with suspects and conduct undercover operations.

The informal nature of IVTS allows them to disguise illicit transactions among the proceeds from cash intensive businesses. Businesses operating with substantial amounts of cash or involving high turnover make it very easy to hide illegal IVTS transactions by creating "black holes": pooling cash among IVTS providers, depositing it at different financial institutions at different times, and/ or using the funds to purchase commodities that then can be traded in the United States or internationally. This process makes matching cash withdrawals or deposits with individual transactions virtually impossible.

Finally, the unconventional settlement between IVTS operators often presents challenges for regulators and law enforcement. The settlement of payments is often unrelated in time to the actual transactions. This makes "following the money trail" much more difficult than traditional financial transactions. This is especially true for IVTS operators who operate in the United States and send funds on behalf of their customers to family and friends located in countries abroad. This continued flow of activity creates a surplus of funds collected by IVTS operators in the United States, while depleting the funds available from "cash pools" available to IVTS operators located in countries abroad who pay out funds to the beneficiaries. Settlement payments must eventually be made between the IVTS operators in order to reconcile existing cash pools that are essential for sustaining IVTS operations in addition to returning a profit for IVTS operators.

The settlement process is executed by IVTS operators utilizing numerous methods that are only limited to what is available within a respective economy. Methods of settling debt may include the physical transport of money, transferring funds or sending checks via traditional

banks, over- and under- invoicing schemes, and countless other methods. A number of recent law enforcement cases suggest that the use of financial institutions is a prevalent method used by IVTS operators located in the United States to remit settlement payments to other IVTS operators located abroad.

## Regulation and Public Policy

FinCEN has issued regulations requiring IVTS to register with FinCEN, effective as of December 2001. Failure to register is a violation of 18 U.S.C. § 1960[79] and 31 U.S.C § 5322.[80] IVTS do not have to identify themselves as an IVTS; however, if they function as a money transmitter they must provide FinCEN with contact and identification information and file reports on transactions over $3,000, cash and coin received amounting to $10,000 or more, and prescribed suspicious transactions. As with all MSBs, registering these businesses has been a slow and challenging process, particularly in the case of small businesses that offer IVTS services as a sideline to their primary function.

In the aftermath of the September 11 attacks, IVTS have become the subject of heightened regulatory focus around the world.[81]

---

[79] *See* 18 U.S.C. § 1960 ("Whoever knowingly conducts, controls, manages, supervises, directs, or owns all or part of an unlicensed money transmitting business, shall be fined in accordance with this title or imprisoned not more than five years, or both.").

[80] *See generally* "FinCEN Report to Congress in accordance with Section 359 of the USA PATRIOT Act." Accessed at: http://www.fincen.gov/hawalarptfinal11222002.pdf.

[81] The FATF SR VI Interpretative Note underscores the need to bring all money or value transfer services, whether formal or informal, within the ambit of certain minimum legal and regulatory requirements in accordance with the relevant FATF recommendations. FATF, *Interpretative Note to Special Recommendation VI: Alternative Remittance.* Accessed at: http://www.fatf-gafi.org/dataoecd/53/34/34262291.pdf.

## Chapter 5
# BULK CASH SMUGGLING

Federal law enforcement agencies believe bulk cash smuggling may be on the rise due in part to increasingly effective AML policies and procedures at U.S. financial institutions. The increased transparency associated with transferring funds through U.S. banks and MSBs is apparently a factor in money launderers moving illicit funds out of the country to jurisdictions with lax or complicit financial institutions or to fund criminal enterprises. Smugglers conceal cash in vehicles, commercial shipments, express packages, luggage, and on private aircraft or boats. Law enforcement is aware of the problem, but has concentrated resources on screening inbound, rather than outbound, passengers and cargo in this era of heightened caution about terrorism.

Cash associated with illicit narcotics typically flows out of the United States across the southwest border into Mexico, retracing the route that illegal drugs follow when entering the United States.[82] Upon leaving the country, cash may stay in Mexico, continue on to a number of other countries, or make a U-turn and head back into the United States as a deposit by a bank or *casa de cambio*. Illicit funds leaving the United States also flow into Canada, which, like Mexico, is a source of illegal narcotics. The extent to which cash smuggled out of the United States is derived from criminal activity other than the sale of illegal drugs is not known. Other cash-intensive sources of illicit income include alien smuggling, bribery, contraband smuggling, extortion, fraud, illegal gambling, kidnapping, prostitution, and tax evasion.

One source of data on currency seizures is the El Paso Intelligence Center (EPIC), which was established in 1974 to assist federal, state, and local law enforcement regarding the movement of illegal drugs and immigration violations on the southwest border. EPIC has three databases, categorized by mode of transport, that track currency seizure information submitted by participating law enforcement agencies:

- **Operation Pipeline** records seizures made from private cars and trucks;

- **Operation Convoy** records highway seizures involving commercial vehicles; and

- **Operation Jetway** records seizures from airports, train and bus stations, package shipment facilities (i.e. FedEx and UPS), United States Post Offices, and airport hotels and motels.

EPIC seizure data from 2001 through 2003 indicates seized currency was most often coming from California, Illinois, New York, and Texas (see Table 8) and was heading to Arizona, California, Florida, and Texas (see Table 9). There is no way to know what proportion of the seized funds was generated through drug trafficking; however, law enforcement believes much, if not most, of the seized cash does represent drug proceeds.[83]

**Bulk Cash Smuggling to Canada**

The cycle of illegal drugs coming into the U.S. and illicit proceeds flowing out is not limited to the southwest border. Operation Candy Box, concluded in March 2004, illustrates the global scope of drug supply into the U.S. and corresponding destinations for illicit proceeds. Operation Candy Box was a three-year Drug Enforcement Administration and ICE investigation that targeted a Vietnamese MDMA[1] and marijuana distribution organization operating in the U.S. and Canada. MDMA powder was imported from the Netherlands and formed into tablets in clandestine labs in Canada. Approximately $5 million a month in drug proceeds was laundered in Canada coming in from the U.S. as bulk cash or laundered through a network of Vietnamese-owned money remitters and travel agencies.[2] It is interesting to note that the defendant charged with money laundering received a stiffer sentence than the defendants charged with narcotics violations.

[1] *MDMA (3-4 methylenedioxymethamphetamine) is a synthetic, psychoactive drug chemically similar to the stimulant methamphetamine and the hallucinogen mescaline. Street names include Ecstasy, Adam, XTC, hug, beans, and love drug.*
[2] *International Narcotics Control Strategy Report, March 2005; http://www.state.gov/p/inl/rls/nrcrpt/2005/vol1/html/42361.htm.*

---

[82] Mexican criminal groups exert more influence over drug trafficking in the U.S. than any other group, accounting for most of the cocaine, and much of the heroin, marijuana, and methamphetamine available in U.S. drug markets (*Source*: National Drug Intelligence Center, National Drug Threat Assessment, 2005).

[83] National Drug Threat Assessment 2005, National Drug Intelligence Center. Accessed at: http://www.usdoj.gov/ndic/pubs11/12620/money.htm#Top.

U.S. Immigration and Customs Enforcement (ICE) plays a key role in investigating bulk cash seizures made by Customs and Border Protection (CBP) and state and local law enforcement. CBP and ICE seizure and arrest data is captured in the Treasury Enforcement Communications System II (TECS II). TECS II is one of world's largest databases containing over a decade of data relating to domestic and international financial crimes.[84]

From 2001 through February 2005 ICE agents arrested more than 260 individuals for bulk cash smuggling violations. Approximately 20% of the arrests resulted from seizures not at a border or port of entry but in the interior of the United States. In addition, ICE and CBP have seized a combined total of more than $107 million in cases where bulk cash smuggling was charged.

## CASE EXAMPLE 4

**Smugglers' Route: U.S. Interstate 59**

Illicit proceeds destined for Mexico often are transported through Texas on U.S. Interstate 59, which extends from the US/Mexican border at Laredo to Houston and then north to other markets throughout the Midwest. Currently, a portion of U.S. Interstate 59 is slated to become part of U.S. Interstate 69. The proposed new highway will create a direct corridor between the U.S.-Mexico border and the U.S.-Canada border. On February 8, 2005, Texas Department of Public Safety (DPS) troopers seized $2.3 million following a vehicle stop along U.S. Interstate 59 north of Nacogdoches. A Texas DPS trooper stopped the driver of a southbound tractor-trailer for a speeding violation. The driver, who was hauling boxes of frozen chicken, appeared to be nervous; his driver's log indicated that this was his first trip for the company. A search of the vehicle revealed a hidden compartment in the refrigerated trailer, and an inspection of the compartment uncovered the currency. DPS officers confiscated the currency, and the driver was arrested on state money laundering charges. This was the fourth largest traffic stop seizure of currency in Texas DPS history[1].

[1] *Narcotics Digest Weekly, National Drug Intelligence Center; Volume 4, Number 10, March 8, 2005, Product No. 2005-R0485-010.*

Bulk cash once it crosses the southwest border can take a number of routes, including:

- Individuals depositing the cash into Mexican banks or *casas de cambio* and then wiring it back into the United States;

- Complicit Mexican financial institutions repatriating the cash to the United States via cash couriers or armored cars, depositing the funds into correspondent accounts;

- Smugglers moving the money on to Venezuela, Panama, Costa Rica, or other Latin American countries where it can be used to pay for goods – both legitimate and illicit – for the black market in Colombia; and,

- Individuals moving the funds to offshore jurisdictions with heightened bank secrecy protections.

SARs filed by U.S. financial institutions tend to support the view that some of the cash smuggled out of the United States to Mexico is immediately repatriated. SARs have reported patterns of large wire transactions ($1.5 million or more per transaction) to U.S. payees from Mexican money exchange houses and other financial institutions. This was reported in the first SAR Activity Review in October 2000, providing an early indication that Mexican criminal groups had raised their profile in drug trafficking in the United States, which correspondingly indicated an increased threat of money laundering activity linked to Mexico.

The ICE attaché in Mexico City, in coordination with Mexican authorities, is conducting investigations into the smuggling of bulk cash from the United States into Mexico and onward to Central and South America. Three separate outbound operations conducted at Benito Juarez International Airport in Mexico City resulted in the seizure of over $21 million and the arrest of over 50 individuals.

---

[84] These include violations of 31 USC § 5316 (failure to file a report of international transportation of currency or monetary instruments), 31 USC § 5332 (bulk cash smuggling), 18 USC § 1956 (laundering of monetary instruments) and 18 USC § 1957 (money laundering in property derived from specified unlawful activity).

## Vulnerabilities

Cash can be smuggled out of the United States through the 317 official land, sea, and air ports of entry (POE), and any number of unofficial routes out of the country along the Canadian and Mexican borders. The United States shares a 3,987 mile border with Canada and a 1,933 mile border with Mexico.

The northern border recorded 77 million individual crossings and 37 million vehicle crossings in 2004. In addition to individuals carrying cash out of the country or hiding it in vehicles, any of the Canada-bound shipping containers involved in commercial trade could contain illicit cash. Canada is the largest U.S. trading partner with $446 billion in merchandise trade last year. Canada is also a major source of marijuana — "B.C. Bud" or British Colombian and other hydroponic high-potency marijuana which commands a selling price of nearly ten times that of Mexican marijuana.

The southern border has five times more traffic than the northern border. There are 35 official ports of entry on the U.S. border with Mexico and some 1 million individuals cross over daily.[85] Mexico ranks right behind Canada as a U.S. trading partner with $267 billion in merchandise trade last year, creating ample opportunity to smuggle cash out of the country in shipping containers.

A significant amount of cash can be moved relatively easily, despite the bulk. Each note of U.S. currency weighs approximately one gram and 454 grams make a pound. Each bill is .0043 inches thick. One million dollars in $20 bills would be six stacks of bills each three feet high with a total weight of a little over 100 pounds.[86] Most airlines have a carry-on weight limit of 40 pounds and a checked baggage limit of 70 pounds. Because of both its bulk and its weight, the challenge in moving bulk cash is either to use large containers (e.g., commercial shipping containers or specialized compartments in vehicles) or split it up among many couriers. Using many couriers has the added advantage of mitigating the risk of loss should one or more couriers be stopped.

Transporting cash out of the U.S. is so commonplace that many criminals do not take any elaborate measures to conceal the currency. (See Table 10) In FY2002 and FY2003, CBP seized almost a quarter of a billion dollars that they characterized as being "unconcealed." When cash is concealed, the methods can be ingenious including false compartments in vehicles and luggage, special garments designed to hold currency that are worn under clothing, and cash packaged and wrapped to look like gifts.

Bulk cash smugglers are well aware of law enforcement's resource constraints at the border and usually cross at busy sites, carefully timing and coordinating crossings. Despite the relative ease of smuggling cash across official border crossing points, there is ample evidence drug, currency, and alien smugglers use other routes as well. Evidence from the apprehension of illegal aliens emphasizes how porous the U.S./Mexican border can be: "U.S. officials made 1.1 million apprehensions along the southern border last year, a 24% increase over the year before. It is unclear whether the rising apprehensions signify that more people are trying to cross or that a greater percentage are being caught. But experts in both countries estimate that perhaps 500,000 or more still make it through each year."[87]

In addition to overland routes between the United States and Mexico, smugglers also use tunnels. From 1990 through March 1, 2005, law enforcement officials discovered 33 tunnels along the U.S.-Mexican border, 21 of which were discovered in Arizona. Nineteen extended from various locations in Nogales, Mexico, to the adjacent city of Nogales, Arizona. Many of the tunnels were located near ports of entry at the border and consisted of passageways linked to storm/sewer drains with entrances concealed in residences or businesses. Two tunnels discovered in Nogales, Arizona had entrances hidden inside churches.[88]

---

[85] Fisk, Daniel W., Deputy Assistant Secretary State for Western Hemisphere Affairs, Statement Before the Senate Committee on Foreign Relations, April 6, 2005.

[86] Bureau of Engraving and Printing. Accessed at: http://www.moneyfactory.com/section.cfm/19.

[87] Sullivan, Kevin, "An Often Crossed Line in the Sand," The Washington Post, March 7, 2005, p.1.

[88] Narcotics Digest Weekly, National Drug Intelligence Center, Volume 4, Number 14, April 5, 2005, Product No. 2005- R0485-014.

[89] Weiss, Martin A., Terrorist Financing: Current Efforts and Policy Issues for Congress, Congressional Research Service, Order Code RL32539, August 20, 2004.

Bulk cash smugglers have an unlimited number of options available to move cash by land, sea, and air out of the United States, but law enforcement resources are limited. As of Oct. 2004, CBP had only 17 currency detector dogs assigned to 14 ports of entry to assist in interdiction efforts.[89] CBP's Canine Enforcement Program was responsible for seizures of U.S. currency worth $27.9 million in FY2003. However, CBP's mission extends far beyond interdicting currency smuggling. On the average day, CBP examines 1.3 million arriving passengers, 410,000 vehicles, seizes $500,000 in currency and 4 tons of narcotics, arrests 2600 fugitives or violators, while facilitating commercial trade and collecting $52 million in duty.[90]

## Regulation and Public Policy

Prior to the passage of the USA PATRIOT Act, an individual smuggling bulk quantities of cash was subject to criminal penalties and/or jail time[91] or civil penalties[92] for the failure to file a Report of International Transportation of Currency or Monetary Instruments (CMIR) as required by 31 U.S.C. § 5316 and 31 C.F.R. § 103.23. The unreported currency was also subject to criminal or civil forfeiture.[93] Forfeiture authority was curtailed by the 1998 case United States v. Bajakajian, in which the U.S. Supreme Court held that forfeiture in a case involving a CMIR violation is subject to the Excessive Fines Clause of the Eighth Amendment.[94] The Court concluded that, given the relatively insignificant nature of the defendant's reporting violation in that case, the forfeiture of over $300,000 in unreported funds would be unconstitutionally excessive. The outcome of the case impaired law enforcement's use of forfeiture for a reporting violation as a method to deter the smuggling of criminal proceeds into or out of the United States.

Aware of this impediment, Congress made the act of bulk cash smuggling itself a criminal offense with Section 371 of the USA PATRIOT Act of 2001 (31 U.S.C. § 5332).[95] Bulk cash smuggling is defined as concealing and smuggling or attempting to smuggle more than $10,000 in currency or monetary instruments into or out of the United States with the intent to evade the CMIR reporting requirement.[96] Bulk cash smuggling is punishable by imprisonment of not more than five years and forfeiture of all property, real or personal, involved in the offense or traceable to the offense.[97]

To improve bulk cash smuggling interdiction, CBP has developed an Outbound Currency Interdiction Training (OCIT) program. The training includes instruction and practical exercises to provide specialized knowledge in currency interdiction, and has an anti-terrorism component. In FY2003, OCIT trained 56 inspectors.[98]

CBP sets performance targets based on the value of outbound currency seizures, and the effectiveness of targeting individuals and vehicles for examination. Outbound enforcement targeting effectiveness is the total number of positive examinations divided by the total number of targeted examinations conducted.[99] In FY2003 CBP's seizure target was $49 million, and the actual seizure amount was $51.7 million. CBP's outbound targeting effectiveness was 5.74% (the target was 9%). Targeting refers to identifying high-risk passengers or vehicles for examination.

In an effort to enlist and expand support on the Mexican side of the border for currency interdiction, the United States-Mexico Border Partnership was signed in March 2002.[100] The initial bilateral efforts have focused on five major programs:

---

[89] National Drug Threat Assessment 2005.
[91] 31 U.S.C. § 5322(a) or (b).
[92] 31 U.S.C. § 5321(a).
[93] Now codified at 31 U.S.C. § 5317(c).
[94] See United States v. Bajakajian, 524 U.S. 321 (1998).
[95] See Section 371 of the USA PATRIOT Act of 2001 (Congressional findings in paragraph (a)).
[96] 31 U.S.C. § 5332.
[97] 31 U.S.C. § 5317(c).
[98] Weiss, Martin A., Terrorist Financing: Current Efforts and Policy Issues for Congress, Congressional Research Service, Order Code RL32539, August 20, 2004.
[99] For more information see DHS, Performance and Accountability Report FY2003, p. 157.
[100] Fisk, Daniel W., Deputy Assistant Secretary State for Western Hemisphere Affairs, Statement Before the Senate Committee on Foreign Relations, April 6, 2005.

- Vehicle and Cargo Inspection System (VACIS) refers to devices able to scan (x-ray or gamma ray) sealed containers. The United States has ten permanent devices capable of scanning up to a railroad car size vehicle, three mobile VACIS (for moveable truck or car inspection) and three portable x-ray scanners (for inspecting luggage) at seven border crossing sites, international airports, and rail stations. The United States plans to install the VACIS machines along the southern border this year.

- Advanced Passenger Information System (APIS) enables the Mexican authorities to screen passenger manifests of incoming commercial air flights against law enforcement, terrorism, and immigration data banks in both Mexico and the United States. APIS was placed into operation in 2004.

- Secure Electronic Network for Travelers Rapid Inspection (SENTRI) are special land border crossing lanes for expedited inspection of pre-registered, low risk, frequent travelers to reduce inspection loads. CBP now has fully-funded projects underway coordinated on both sides of the border at six principal crossing sites.

- Border Wizard is software the United States uses that creates a simulated model of a border crossing and inspection site as a management tool to analyze traffic flow and resource use. The software is being adapted for Mexico.

- Safety and Training courses for Mexican border law enforcement personnel.

Table 8

Top Ten Origins and Number of Recorded Seizures of Cash and Monetary Instruments (2001–2003)

| 2001 | | 2002 | | 2003 | |
|---|---|---|---|---|---|
| Texas | 140 | Texas | 130 | Texas | 128 |
| California | 122 | California | 126 | California | 115 |
| New York | 122 | New York | 81 | New York | 78 |
| Illinois | 113 | Illinois | 71 | Illinois | 77 |
| Georgia | 76 | Georgia | 56 | Georgia | 59 |
| Ohio | 60 | Ohio | 48 | Florida | 45 |
| Michigan | 57 | Florida | 44 | Ohio | 45 |
| Florida | 48 | Michigan | 43 | Tennessee | 39 |
| Missouri | 48 | Tennessee | 32 | Michigan | 37 |
| North Carolina | 47 | Missouri | 31 | Arizona | 36 |

Table 9

Top Ten Destinations and Number of Recorded Seizures of Cash and Monetary Instruments (2001–2003)

| 2001 | | 2002 | | 2003 | |
|---|---|---|---|---|---|
| California | 328 | Texas | 244 | Texas | 235 |
| Texas | 304 | California | 238 | California | 231 |
| Florida | 115 | Arizona | 89 | Arizona | 99 |
| Arizona | 111 | Florida | 63 | Florida | 58 |
| Illinois | 57 | Unknown | 41 | Georgia | 38 |
| Nevada | 31 | Georgia | 25 | New York | 33 |
| Tennessee | 31 | New York | 25 | Illinois | 28 |
| Georgia | 28 | Illinois | 24 | Tennessee | 22 |
| Maryland | 28 | Tennessee | 21 | Nevada | 21 |
| New York | 25 | Nevada | 18 | Colorado | 19 |
| No State ID | 502 | No State ID | 333 | No State ID | 339 |

Source: El Paso Intelligence Center

Table 10

The data below represents all CBP seizures above $30,000 from FY 2002–FY 2003.

| CBP Data for Currency Concealment Method (2002–2003) | | | | | |
|---|---|---|---|---|---|
| Sorted by Number of Seizures | | | Sorted by $ Amount | | |
| Concealment Method | Number of Seizures | Amount in Millions | Concealment Method | Number of Seizures | Amount in Millions |
| Unconcealed | 561 | $243.0 | Unconcealed | 561 | $243.0 |
| Other bag* | 317 | $50.4 | Other bag* | 317 | $50.4 |
| Suitcase | 199 | $33.4 | Car/Truck | 194 | $37.4 |
| Car/Truck | 194 | $37.4 | Suitcase | 199 | $33.4 |
| Express package | 170 | $31.8 | Express package | 170 | $31.8 |
| On body | 139 | $7.7 | Bus/Train/Cycle | 108 | $30.4 |
| Other | 124 | $23.2 | Other | 124 | $23.2 |
| Bus/Train/Cycle | 108 | $30.4 | Unidentified | 43 | $13.8 |
| Clothing | 86 | $4.0 | Cargo | 15 | $9.9 |
| Box | 45 | $9.1 | Box | 45 | $9.1 |
| Unidentified | 43 | $13.8 | On body | 139 | $7.7 |
| Camper | 30 | $6.3 | Trunk | 14 | $7.1 |
| Cargo | 15 | $9.9 | Camper | 30 | $6.3 |
| Mail parcel | 14 | $4.3 | Mail parcel | 14 | $4.3 |
| Trunk | 14 | $7.1 | Clothing | 86 | $4.0 |
| Body Cavity | 4 | $0.4 | Cargo Container | 2 | $0.7 |
| Vessel | 4 | $0.6 | Vessel | 4 | $0.6 |
| Aircraft | 2 | $0.2 | Body Cavity | 4 | $0.4 |
| Cargo Container | 2 | $0.7 | Aircraft | 2 | $0.2 |

Source: "Detection of Outbound Currency" by Keith A. Daum, et. al., published by the Idaho National Engineering and Environmental Laboratory Special Programs Department, November 2004.

* "Other bag" is any type of bag other than suitcase.

## Chapter 6
# TRADE-BASED MONEY LAUNDERING

Trade-based money laundering encompasses a variety of schemes that enable the cash to be separated from the crime early in the money laundering process. The most common method of trade-based money laundering in the Western Hemisphere is the Black Market Peso Exchange (BMPE), in which Colombian drug traffickers swap illicit dollars in the United States for clean pesos in Colombia. Other methods include manipulating trade documents to over- or underpay for imports and exports, and using criminal proceeds to buy gems or precious metals.

Trade-based money laundering schemes often allow criminals to distance themselves from the money laundering process, complicating law enforcement investigations. Immigration and Customs Enforcement (ICE) analyzes outbound trade data, and financial and payment data, including forms mandated by the BSA – the Currency Transaction Report (CTR), Report of International Transportation of Currency or Monetary Instruments (CMIR), Report of Cash Payments over $10,000 Received in a Trade or Business (Form 8300), and the Suspicious Activity Report (SAR) – in an effort to spot the anomalies that would indicate trade-based money laundering. The Drug Enforcement Administration (DEA) has recently refocused its investigative efforts to address the BMPE as it relates to narcotics money laundering.

### Black Market Peso Exchange

The BMPE emerged in the 1980s as a sophisticated alternative to laundering funds through the United States banking system, and while used primarily in South America and the Caribbean it is most often associated with laundering Colombian drug profits.[101] The BMPE is the largest known money laundering system in the Western Hemisphere, responsible for moving an estimated $5 billion worth of drug proceeds per year from the United States back to Colombia.[102]

The scheme allows drug traffickers to launder their illicit proceeds by exchanging their dollars in the United States for pesos in Colombia without physically moving funds from one country to the other. Money brokers act as intermediaries between the drug traffickers and Colombian businessmen. The money brokers sell the illicit dollars they buy from drug dealers in the United States to Colombian businesses that use the money to pay for U.S. products such as home appliances, consumer electronics, alcohol, tobacco, and used auto parts, which are exported to Colombia and elsewhere. The BMPE has many of the same attributes as the *hawala* system.

The BMPE originally was driven by Colombia's restrictive policies on currency exchange. Access to U.S. dollars is regulated by Colombian law and administered by the central bank. Before the central bank will exchange pesos for dollars, the importer has to demonstrate that government import permits have been obtained, thereby insuring that the applicable Colombian duties and taxes will be collected. Colombian businesses bypass the government levies by dealing with BMPE brokers.[103]

When money brokers take possession of illicit U.S. currency, they keep the funds in the United States, often enlisting individuals to buy money orders with the drug dollars or deposit the money in U.S. bank accounts. As additional drug dollars come in, the money brokers use runners to deposit the cash or smuggle it out of the country and then wire it into the U.S. accounts from foreign banks. The money brokers use those U.S. accounts and money orders to pay for U.S. exports on behalf of their Colombian business clients. The Colombian businesses complete the money laundering cycle, paying for the U.S. dollars they need with pesos in Colombia, and the pesos, in turn, go directly to local drug traffickers who use the money to fund the next narcotics shipment to the United States.

---

[101] Zarate, Juan Carlos, Assistant Secretary Terrorist Financing and Financial Crimes, U.S. Department of the Treasury testimony before the House Financial Services Committee Subcommittee on Oversight and Investigations, February 16, 2005.

[102] Tandy, Karen P., Administrator , Drug Enforcement Administration, testimony before the United States Senate Caucus on International Narcotics Control, March 4, 2004.

[103] Tishler, Bonni, Asst. Commissioner, U.S. Customs Service, testimony before the Senate Caucus on International Narcotics Control, June 21, 1999.

Often U.S. merchants become unwitting accomplices in the money laundering process by accepting payment in funds derived from illegal activity.[104] (See "Operation Meltdown" Case Example.) A telltale sign of money laundering is when the checks, bank wires, or money orders used to pay for U.S. merchandise do not come from individuals or businesses buying the goods but from third parties with no apparent connection to the transaction.[105]

### CASE EXAMPLE 5

**Operation Meltdown**

Operation Meltdown, an ICE case that concluded in 2003, is a complex and ingenious example of the BMPE. Peso brokers created fictional payments for gold bullion imported into the United States from Colombia. The transactions provided cover for the transfer of pesos to Colombian drug suppliers. Actual gold bullion was sent to the U.S. and declared to U.S. Customs to authenticate the payments. To get the gold back to Colombia to repeat the cycle, the bullion was disguised by melting it down and molding it into innocuous objects including wrenches, nuts, and bolts, which were then painted. The drug suppliers received their proceeds in pesos from Colombian merchants. And the merchants, in turn, used the drug money in the United States to pay for U.S. exports to Colombia. New York jewelers participating in the scheme made the payments for the exported U.S. goods on behalf of the Colombian merchants. Operation Meltdown resulted in 20 convictions for money laundering and BSA violations.

An analysis conducted by the NY/NJ HIFCA identified thousands of transactions involving millions of dollars in BMPE activity wired through New York banks in the name of a money exchange business in Uruguay. The beneficiaries of many of the outgoing wires were electronic or computer vendors in Florida.

Several New York bank accounts revealed structured cash deposits, which were subsequently paid out by

check to vendors in Panama. The Colon Free Trade Zone in Panama, where the dollar is the preferred currency, allows companies to export goods tax-free. There are 1,400 companies with assembly plants and warehouses there selling everything from appliances and pharmaceuticals to furniture and toys. Hundreds of millions of dollars have been traced from U.S. accounts to Panama vendors of gold jewelry, electronics, and other goods, which were then shipped to Colombia.[106]

### Alternative Trade-based Money Laundering Schemes

Criminal organizations may resort to a number of alternatives to the BMPE for transferring value into or out of the United States. Each of these schemes relies on the misuse of international trade documents. Among the most frequently encountered schemes are: over- and under-valuation, misclassification, and double invoicing. Each of these schemes is a separate offense that may also be an element of the crime of money laundering.

Two of the most common alternative schemes are over- and under-valuation. An over-valuation scheme involves the presentation of an invoice that overstates the true value of the related merchandise. In this case, the importer pays more for the merchandise than it is truly worth, providing the justification for the importer to move money offshore, ostensibly in payment for the imported goods. An under-valuation scheme is the same thing in reverse. An importer receives merchandise that is worth more than declared in the invoice. When the importer sells the under-valued merchandise, he receives more than the value reflected in the official documentation. If the transferred value represents illicit proceeds, the result is money laundering. In addition to being a money laundering method, businesses have attempted to over- and under-value trade goods in an effort to dodge government trade duties, taxes, or other fees based on the value of the merchandise sent or received.

### Foreign Trade Zones (FTZs)

Foreign Trade Zones (known as Free Trade Zones outside of the United States) are intended to promote manu-

---

[104] *See generally* FinCEN Advisory, Issues 9 & 12. Accessed at: http://www.fincen.gov/advis12.pdf.

[105] 2003 NY/NJ HIFCA Threat Assessment.

[106] Roth, John, Chief of the Asset Forfeiture and Money Laundering Section, Dept. of Justice, testimony before the Committee on Government Reform, Subcommittee on Criminal Justice, Drug Policy, and Human Resources, May 11, 2004.

facturing in the host country, but can also be used to facilitate money laundering. When U.S.-based manufacturers import parts and materials outside of a Foreign Trade Zone (FTZ), they pay import duties based on the value of the finished product rather than the value of the component parts. Operating in an FTZ allows manufacturers to defer, reduce, or even eliminate U.S. Customs duties.[107] There are FTZs throughout the United States in 250 communities handling almost $250 billion in merchandise.[108]

Often, criminal operations within an FTZ involve some type of import/export scheme. False documentation involving fabricated Bills of Lading and fictitious names and addresses are used to misrepresent imports and exports, often with a customs broker who is in collusion with the criminals, "brokering" the documents with CBP.

### Precious Commodities

Precious commodities, gems, and metals can be used as an alternative to cash to transfer value across borders. Like gold and other precious metals, diamonds are attractive to money launderers because they are easily concealed and transported, and because they are mined in remote areas of the world and are virtually untraceable to their original source.[109] Even when diamonds are transported openly, it is relatively easy to mislabel the quality/value of a diamond for money laundering purposes.

There is growing worldwide recognition of the need to scrutinize unusual trade patterns involving commodities. An example is "conflict diamonds" emerging from non-diamond producing West African countries and exported to Belgium. Conflict diamonds are produced by rogue nations that use the proceeds to fund factions opposed to legitimate and internationally recognized governments. In response to the threat posed by conflict diamonds, the Kimberley Process was created to document the

movement of rough stones through the diamond pipeline and to limit trade to participating countries. The Kimberley Process requires that each shipment of rough diamonds being exported and crossing an international border be transported in a tamper-resistant container and be accompanied by a government validated Kimberley Process Certificate, which is uniquely numbered and includes the description of the shipment's contents.[110]

### Vulnerabilities

Individual prosecutions of peso brokers, their agents in the United States, and businesses that buy or receive BMPE dollars have been successful, but have had little effect on the system or Colombian drug trafficking organizations that sell their dollars to the peso brokers. As a consequence, DEA is changing its investigative tactics into BMPE money laundering investigations in an effort to inflict the most damage upon the Colombian sources of drug supply. DEA is also a participant in an ICE-led multi-agency initiative to attack the BMPE as a system rather than on an individual case-by-case basis.[111]

FTZs are vulnerable to money launderers due to a lack of connectivity and automation. When items are shipped through private sector package delivery services they can be tracked electronically from pick up to drop off, but no similar system exists for U.S. Customs to track commercial goods in real-time moving into or out of FTZs.

In a case involving money coming into the United States, the FTZ in Los Angeles indicated cargo that had come in from the FTZ in Miami had left the country following receipt of payment from the importer. Law enforcement, however, later found the paperwork to be fraudulent and the cargo diverted to Kentucky. In a case involving money leaving the United States, more than $100,000 was sent to a bank in Cyprus for merchandise due to be imported into a North Carolina FTZ. Law enforcement determined the corresponding paperwork

---

[107] *See* The National Association of Foreign Trade Zones, *Benefits of FTZs*. Accessed at: http://www.naftz.org/index_categories.php/ftzs/5.

[108] *See* U.S. Foreign-Trade Zones Board, *Information Summary*. Accessed at: http://ia.ita.doc.gov/ftzpage/info/summary.html.

[109] Yager, Loren, Director, International Affairs and Trade, U.S. General Accounting Office., Testimony before the Subcommittee on Oversight of Government Management, Restructuring and the District of Colombia, Committee on Governmental Affairs, U.S. Senate, February 13, 2002.

[110] Zarate, Juan Carlos, Assistant Secretary Terrorist Financing and Financial Crimes, U.S. Department of the Treasury testimony before the House Financial Services Committee Subcommittee on Oversight and Investigations, February 16, 2005.

[111] Karen P. Tandy, Administrator, Drug Enforcement Administration, testimony before the United States Senate Caucus on International Narcotics Control, March 4, 2004.

never accurately accounted for any merchandise really changing hands.

The Kimberley Process represents an advance in counteracting the trade in conflict diamonds, yet the procedures were not designed specifically to combat money laundering or other financial crimes associated with diamonds. For example, the trade in rough diamonds and the mixing of parcels before being imported into a country for finishing and sale is a recognized vulnerability. There are reports that in some locations Kimberley certificates can be purchased on the black market. The latest Kimberley Process plenary meeting that took place in Canada in October 2004, however, noted significant progress in the implementation of the Kimberley Process Certification scheme. Kimberley Process participants now encompass the overwhelming majority of the producers and traders in rough diamonds.[112]

## Regulation and Public Policy

In June 2005, FinCEN issued an interim final rule extending the AML compliance program requirements under the BSA to "dealers" in precious metals, stones, or jewels.[113] Dealers are required to have an AML compliance program documented in writing and approved by senior management. The AML program must incorporate policies, procedures, and internal controls based upon the dealer's assessment of the money laundering and terrorist financing risks associated with its line of business.[114] Dealers are also encouraged to adopt procedures for voluntarily filing suspicious activity reports. Finally, dealers are separately obligated to report on a Form 8300 the receipt of cash or certain non-cash instruments totaling more than $10,000 in one transaction or two or more related transactions.[115]

The ICE Financial and Trade Investigations Division is home to the Trade Transparency Unit (TTU), a joint initiative of the Departments of Homeland Security, State, and Treasury. The TTU was created by ICE to target and eliminate vulnerabilities in transnational trade that can be exploited by criminal organizations to earn, move, and store illicit proceeds. Under appropriate agreements, ICE and a foreign government exchange trade data. The TTU uses a data mining software application, called the Data Analysis and Research for Trade Transparency System (DARTTS), to sift through trade data, passenger manifests, BSA filings, and immigration data looking for anomalies that might indicate BMPE activity. DARTTS is also effective in identifying under- and over-valuation schemes, and can be used by governments to identify and recover revenue that is denied them through the workings of these types of fraud.

One good example of trade transparency in action is the joint efforts of ICE and the government of Colombia under Plan Colombia. ICE Special Agents are detailed to the Colombian Customs and Tax Authority, and computers and training have been provided to assist in the analysis of United States and Colombian trade data, and to develop leads for investigation. ICE is attempting to duplicate the results of Plan Colombia with other Central and South American countries.[116]

---

[112] Zarate, Juan Carlos, Assistant Secretary Terrorist Financing and Financial Crimes, U.S. Department of the Treasury testimony before the House Financial Services Committee Subcommittee on Oversight and Investigations, February 16, 2005.

[113] See 31 CFR 103.140 (70 FR 33702 (2005)). "Dealers" are defined as those who have purchased and sold more than $50,000 in covered goods during the preceding year.

[114] See 31 CFR 103.140(c)(1).

[115] See 26 U.S.C. 6050I and 31 CFR 103.30.

[116] Forman, Marcy M., Deputy Assistant Director, Financial Investigations, Immigration and Customs Enforcement, Department of Homeland Security, testimony before the House Government Reform Committee Subcommittee on Criminal Justice Drug Policy and Human Resources, May 11, 2004.

## Chapter 7
# INSURANCE COMPANIES

Life, health, and accident insurance generate more than half a trillion dollars in premiums and contract revenue annually for U.S. insurers. Much of this revenue stream actually comes from the sale of annuities. In fact, according to the National Association of Insurance Commissioners (NAIC), "the primary business of life/health insurance companies is no longer traditional life insurance, but the underwriting of annuities — contracts that guarantee a fixed or variable payment over a given period of time."[117] While whole and term life insurance policies remain an important part of the business, insurance agents and brokers are now often investment advisers selling a variety of financial products. The expansion from insurance policies to investment products has substantially increased the money laundering threat posed by the insurance industry.

Recently, life insurers have developed products that offer a variety of investment options generating fixed or variable returns. These investment products are marketed as part of a diversified portfolio, often with tax benefits. The introduction of investment products to the insurance portfolio has broadened the potential customer base for insurers and agents and has created new transaction patterns. For example, a client with traditional insurance coverage might have had the fixed monthly premium automatically debited from a bank account; now, with an eye toward investment returns, that same client could choose to invest varying amounts monthly, or a single lump sum, potentially delivering cash to the agent.

A number of money laundering methods have been used to exploit the insurance sector, primarily term life insurance policies and annuity products. Money launderers exploit the fact that insurance products are often sold by independent brokers and agents who do not work directly for the insurance companies. These intermediaries may have little know-how or incentive to screen clients or question payment methods. In some cases, agents take advantage of their intermediary status to collude with criminals against insurers to perpetrate fraud or facilitate money laundering.

An insurance company may offer its products through a number of different distribution channels. Some insurers sell their products directly to the insured. Other companies employ agents, who may either be "captive" or independent. Captive agents represent only one insurance company; independent agents may represent a variety of insurance carriers. Insurance may also be purchased through third parties such as financial planners or investment advisors (all of whom must be licensed insurance agents). Some companies and agents offer policies via the Internet.

## Vulnerabilities

Life insurance policies that can be cashed in are an inviting money laundering vehicle because criminals are able to put "dirty" money in and take "clean" money out in the form of an insurance company check. An alternative typology is to borrow against a life insurance policy that is funded with illicit proceeds. Similarly, annuity contracts allow a money launderer to exchange illicit funds for an immediate or deferred "clean" income stream. These vulnerabilities generally do not exist in products offered by property and casualty insurers, or by title or health insurers.

Even when insurers have AML guidance in place, agents who sell insurance policies and investment contracts often are not employed directly by the insurer or service provider, which can make it difficult for companies to ensure their AML policies and procedures are followed. Further complicating AML practices, the policyholder, or purchaser of an insurance contract, may not be the beneficiary or even the subject of the insurance coverage. The potential for multiple parties to be involved in a single contract makes it difficult to perform customer due diligence.

Money laundering through insurance has been generally confined to life insurance products although the actual typologies vary significantly. In one case, federal law enforcement agencies discovered Colombian drug cartels were using drug proceeds to buy life insurance policies, which were subsequently liquidated with the cash value transferred to an offshore jurisdiction. The cash surrender value of a life insurance policy is often much less than the amount invested because of liquidation penalties, particularly if the policy has only been in existence for a few years. But from the drug traffickers' perspective, the liquidation penalty is, in effect, a cost of doing business.[118]

In another case conducted by ICE, illicit drug proceeds were used to purchase three term life insurance policies in Austin, Texas, followed shortly afterward by an attempt to cash in the policies.[119] Federal law enforcement agencies report similar cases involving money laundering through the purchase of variable annuity contracts.

A major ICE investigation into Eagle Star Life, based in the Isle of Man, with an office in Miami, was identified through information received in a narcotics smuggling investigation as issuing policies paid for with drug proceeds. The suspicious policies were established from 1995 through 2003 by one "master broker" who operated in Colombia and other South American countries. The policies were funded in several ways. In many instances, a large wire transfer was sent to the insurer on instructions from the broker. Once received, the broker would direct the allocation of funds to various policies. Eagle Star also received payments via third-party checks and structured money orders. Most alarming is evidence that some policies were paid for with funds from brokers' commission accounts. In this scenario, the brokers accepted cash from the client in Colombia and credited the client's policy with funds from the brokers' business operating account or from commission checks.

## Regulation and Public Policy

The insurance industry in the United States is currently subject to state rather than federal regulation. State regulation focuses primarily on safety and soundness rather than AML. However, FinCEN, pursuant to the BSA, is promulgating AML regulations for the industry.

States oversee the organization and capitalization of insurance companies, permissible investments, licensing of companies and agents, and the form and content of policies. However, there is no consistency across the state regulatory regimes. States vary on how examinations are structured, how many examinations are performed, and how examiners are trained. As a result, states report they find it difficult to depend on other states' oversight of companies' market behavior.[120]

Some states have subjected insurance companies to AML statutes. According to an unpublished survey conducted by the National Association of Insurance Carriers, thirty-eight states have money laundering statutes, twenty-one have currency reporting requirements, and one has a suspicious activity reporting requirement.[121]

FinCEN issued two sets of final rules for the insurance industry in 2005, the first covering minimum standards for AML programs and the second covering suspicious activity reporting requirements.[122] The final rules apply to insurance companies that issue or underwrite certain products that present a high degree of risk for money laundering or the financing of terrorism or other illicit activity. The insurance products subject to these rules include:

- Permanent life insurance policies, other than group life insurance policies;

- Annuity contracts, other than group annuity contracts; and

- Any other insurance products with cash value or investment features.

The AML rule requires insurance companies offering covered insurance products to establish programs that include, at a minimum, the development of internal policies, procedures, and controls; the designation of a compliance officer; and ongoing employee training program; and, an independent audit function.

---

[118] *See* <u>United States v. The Contents of Account No. 400941058 at JP Morgan Chase Bank</u>, New York, NY, Mag. Docket No. 02-1163 (SDNY 2002) (warrent of seizure).

[119] *See* <u>In the Matter of Seizure of the Cash Value and Advance Premium Deposit Funds</u>, Case No. 2002-5506-00007 (W. D. Tex. 2002).

[120] United States General Accounting Office, Insurance Regulation: Preliminary Views on States' Oversight of Insurers' Market Behavior, GAO-03-738T, May 6, 2003.

[121] 67 FR 64067.

[122] Financial Crimes Enforcement Network; Amendment to the Bank Secrecy Act Regulations -- Anti-Money Laundering Programs for Insurance Companies, RIN 1506-AA70, Nov. 3, 2005 and Financial Crimes Enforcement Network; Amendment to the Bank Secrecy Act Regulations- Requirement That Insurance Companies Report Suspicious Transactions, RIN 1506-AA36, Nov. 3, 2005.

## Chapter 8

# SHELL COMPANIES AND TRUSTS

Legal jurisdictions, whether states within the United States or entities elsewhere, that offer strict secrecy laws, lax regulatory and supervisory regimes, and corporate registries that safeguard anonymity are obvious targets for money launderers. A handful of U.S. states offer company registrations with cloaking features – such as minimal information requirements and limited oversight – that rival those offered by offshore financial centers. Delaware, Nevada, and Wyoming are often cited as the most accommodating jurisdictions in the United States for the organization of these legal entities.

The use of bearer shares, nominee shareholders, and nominee directors function to mask ownership in a corporate entity. While these mechanisms were devised to serve legitimate purposes, they can also be used by money launderers to evade scrutiny.

In general, shell companies have no physical presence other than a mailing address, employ no one, and produce nothing. One controversial but legitimate function for shell companies is to serve as a holding company for intellectual property rights. When franchisees or licensees are billed for their use of intellectual property, such as a brand name or trademark, earnings are shifted to the location of the holding company which affects where earnings are recognized and taxes are paid.

Intermediaries, called nominee incorporation services (NIS), establish U.S. shell companies and bank accounts on behalf of foreign clients. NIS may be located in the United States or off-shore. Corporate lawyers in the United States often use NIS to organize companies on behalf of their domestic and foreign clients because such services can efficiently organize legal entities in any state. NIS must comply with applicable state and federal procedures as well as any specific bank requirements. Those laws and procedures dictate what information NIS must share about the owners of a legal entity. Money launderers have also utilized NIS to hide their identities. By hiring a firm to serve as an intermediary between themselves and the licensing jurisdiction and the bank, a company's beneficial owners may avoid disclosing their identities in state corporate filings and in the documentation used to open corporate bank accounts.

Several mechanisms operate to provide corporate entities with additional anonymity. Bearer shares are negotiable instruments that accord ownership of a company to the person who possesses the share certificate. Such share certificates do not contain the name of the shareholder and are not registered, with the possible exception of their serial numbers. Accordingly, these shares provide for a high level of anonymity and are easily negotiable.

Nominee shareholders can also be used in privately-held companies to shield beneficial ownership information. The allowance of nominee shareholders undermines the usefulness of the shareholder register or the shareholder list because the shareholder of record may not be the ultimate beneficial owner. Similarly, nominee directors and companies serving as directors of a legal entity may conceal the identity of those persons controlling the company.

Trusts separate legal ownership from beneficial ownership and are useful when assets are given to minors or individuals who are incapacitated. The trust creator, or settlor, transfers legal ownership of the assets to a trustee, which can be an individual or a corporation. The trustee fiduciary manages the assets on behalf of the beneficiary based on the terms of the trust deed.

Although trusts have many legitimate applications, they can also be misused for illicit purposes. Trusts enjoy a greater degree of privacy and autonomy than other corporate vehicles, as virtually all jurisdictions recognizing trusts do not require registration or central registries and there are few authorities charged with overseeing trusts. In most jurisdictions, no disclosure of the identity of the beneficiary or the settlor is made to authorities. Accordingly, trusts can conceal the identity of the beneficial owner of assets and, as will be discussed below, can be abused for money laundering purposes, particularly in the layering and integration stages.

## Vulnerabilities

Legal entities such as shell companies and trusts are used globally for legitimate business purposes, but because of their ability to hide ownership and mask financial details they have become popular tools for money launderers.

The use of these legal structures for money laundering is well-established. The United Nations noted in a 1998 report that "the principal forms of abuse of secrecy have shifted from individual bank accounts to corporate bank accounts and then to trust and other corporate forms that can be purchased readily without even the modest initial and ongoing due diligence that is exercised in the banking sector."[123]

The competition among certain states to attract legal entities to their jurisdictions has created a "race to the bottom," and a real money laundering threat. (See Figure 5) While they are often used for legitimate purposes, bearer shares, nominee shareholders, and trusts also provide money launderers with the tools to hide their identity from financial institutions and law enforcement.

As an example, a Delaware-registered company may be owned by a national of any jurisdiction, regardless of his or her place of residence. The company can be operated and managed worldwide, and is not required to report any assets. Eastern European and Russian law enforcement agencies have expressed concern that regional criminal organizations were abusing Delaware shell companies for money laundering.[124] And German prosecutors have reportedly complained that the secrecy inherent in Delaware's regime for legal entities has hindered investigations into suspicious financial activity.[125] But, Delaware is not the most permissive jurisdiction in the United States with regard to company formation. Both Nevada and Wyoming permit companies to have bearer shares and nominee shareholders, which Delaware does not.

The FBI has found that certain NIS form corporate entities, open full-service bank accounts for those entities,

and act as the registered agent to accept service of legal process on behalf of those entities in a jurisdiction in which the entities have no physical presence. An NIS can accomplish this without ever having to identify beneficial ownership on company formation, registration, or bank account documents. The FBI believes that U.S. shell companies and bank accounts arranged by certain NIS firms are being used to launder as much as $36 billion a year from the former Soviet Union. It is not clear whether these NIS firms are complicit in the money laundering abuse.

Several international NIS firms have formed partnerships or marketing alliances with U.S. banks to offer financial services such as Internet banking and wire transfer capabilities to shell companies and non-U.S. citizens. The FBI reports that the U.S. banks participating in these marketing alliances open accounts through intermediaries without requiring the actual account holder's physical presence, accepting by mail copies of passport photos, utility bills, and other identifying information.[126]

FinCEN reports that 397 SARs were filed between April 1996[127] and January 2004 involving shell companies, Eastern European countries,[128] and the use of correspondent bank accounts.[129] The aggregate violation amount reported in those 397 SARs totaled almost $4 billion.

The State of New York Banking Department recently noted that Suspicious Activity Reports filed by New York banks indicate an increase in the volume of shell company wire transfer activity through high-risk correspondent bank accounts, both in terms of dollar amounts and the number of transactions.[130] These reports indicate that money is passing through correspondent accounts

---

[123] United Nations Office for Drug Control and Crime Prevention, "Financial Havens, Banking Secrecy and Money-Laundering," 1998, p. 57. Accessed at: http://www.cf.ac.uk/socsi/whoswho/levi-laundering.pdf.

[124] Simpson, Glenn R., Laundering Queries Focus on Delaware, Wall Street Journal, Sept. 30, 2004.

[125] Crawford, David, German Officials Fault U.S. on Money-Laundering Woes, Wall Street Journal, June 18, 2003.

[126] In addition to furnishing shell companies with bank accounts, intermediaries sometimes set up shell banks – foreign banks that do not maintain a physical presence in any country – that are never licensed with a regulatory authority. Such shell banks customarily attempt to pass themselves off as operating brick-and-mortar banks and gain access to the U.S. banking system through "nested" correspondent accounts. *See supra* Chapter 2, "Banking," for more information.

[127] The date financial institutions were mandated to file Suspicious Activity Reports

[128] The eastern European countries that were identified in Suspicious Activity Report narratives with shell companies included Armenia, Belarus, Bulgaria, Croatia, Cyprus, Czech Republic, Estonia, Georgia, Greece, Kazakhstan, Latvia, Lithuania, Moldova, Poland, Romania, Russia, Slovenia, Turkey, Turkmenistan, Ukraine, Uzbekistan, and Yugoslavia.

[129] During this time period a total of approximately 1.5 million SARs were filed.

[130] Financial Crimes Enforcement Network, Suspicious Activity Review, Issue 7, August 2004.

established for Eastern European banks.

Trusts often constitute the final layer of anonymity for those seeking to conceal their identity. Recent changes in the trust laws of some jurisdictions have aided money launderers in their use of trusts to conceal identity and to perpetrate fraud. In certain jurisdictions, such as the Cook Islands, Nevis, and Niue, the trust laws no longer require the names of the settlor and the beneficiaries to be placed in the trust deed, permit settlors to retain control over the trust, and allow trusts to be revocable and of unlimited duration. In addition, the amended trust laws typically permit the trust deed to include a "flee clause," a provision triggered by the occurrence of certain events that directs the assets of the trust to be moved to another jurisdiction and new trustees to be appointed.

## Regulation and Public Policy

Trust companies are defined as "financial institutions" under the Bank Secrecy Act. Shell companies are not specifically listed in the BSA, but could be regulated under the BSA under one of the two catch-all provisions of 31 USC 5312(a), given an appropriate record.

## A Side by Side Comparison of Wyoming and Nevada and Delaware

Figure 2

| Benefits | Nevada | Wyoming | Delaware |
|---|:---:|:---:|:---:|
| Minimal annual fees | | X | |
| One-person company is allowed | X | X | X |
| Stockholders are not revealed to the State | X | X | X |
| No annual report is required until the anniversary of the incorporation date | | X | |
| Unlimited stock is allowed, of any par value | | X | X |
| Bearer stock can be used | X | X | |
| Nominee shareholders are allowed | X | X | |
| Share certificates are not required | | X | |
| Minimal initial filing fees | | X | |
| No minimum capital requirements | X | X | X |
| Meetings may be held anywhere | X | X | X |
| Officers, directors, employees and agents are statutorily indemnified | X | X | |
| Continuance procedure (allows Wyoming to adopt a company formed in another state) | | X | |
| Doesn't collect corporate income tax information to share with the IRS | X | X | |

Copyright 1994–2005 by Corporations Today, Inc. Accessed at: http://www.corporationstoday.com/compare.html#compare.

## Chapter 9
# CASINOS

More than $800 billion was wagered at approximately 845 casinos and card clubs in the United States in 2003, accounting for approximately 85 percent of the total amount of money wagered for all legal gaming activities throughout the country.[131]  In addition to gaming, casinos offer their largely transient customer base a broad array of financial services, such as deposit and credit accounts, funds transfers, check cashing, and currency exchange services, that are similar to those offered by depository institutions and other types of financial institutions.  As high-volume cash businesses, casinos are susceptible to money laundering as well as many other financial crimes and were the first

non-bank financial institutions required to develop AML compliance programs.[132]

The most notable development in this field is the striking growth of Native American casinos, which have enjoyed annual double-digit revenue growth for the last ten years (See Chart 1).  These tribal casinos are moving rapidly from relative obscurity within the casino industry to a prominent position with ample potential for money laundering and other types of financial crimes.  The regulatory structure of the tribal gaming industry is intricate, with somewhat overlapping layers of responsibility at the tribal, state, and federal levels.

In 2004, casino gambling, including commercial casinos – both land-based and riverboat – tribal casinos, card rooms and racinos[133] was legal in 34 states and 3 other jurisdictions (*i.e.*, Puerto Rico, the U.S. Virgin Islands, and Tinian) and some 200 counties.[134]  According to the American Gaming Association, Nevada leads the nation as the state with the highest casino revenue with $9.625 billion in 2003.

There are 567 federally recognized Indian Tribes (half are in Alaska), and 223 of them operate 411 gaming facilities in 28 states.[135]  Of these, 307 are considered casino operations (the remainder are basically bingo halls).  Collectively, tribal casinos took in $18.5 billion in revenue last year, twice the amount generated by Nevada casinos.[136]  If the tribal gaming industry were a single company, rather than 307 casinos, it would rank near the top 100 corporations in America.  Tribal gaming interests have what is currently the largest casino in the United States, Foxwoods Resort and Casino, located in Mashantucket, Connecticut and owned by the

Chart 1

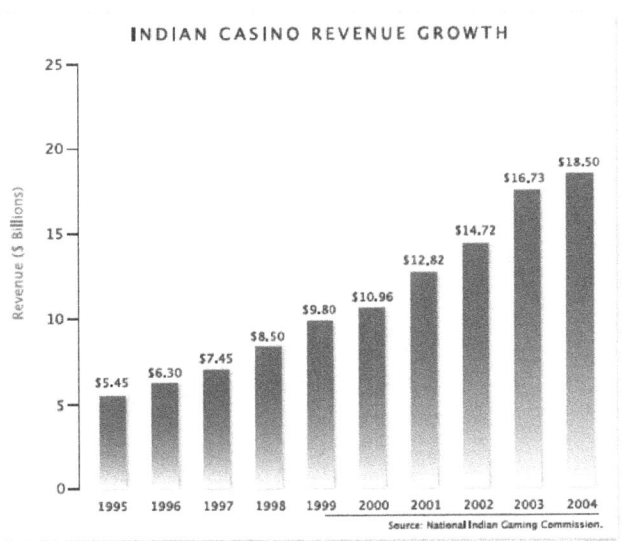

INDIAN CASINO REVENUE GROWTH

Source: National Indian Gaming Commission.

---

[131] FinCEN SAR Activity Review, Issue 8, April 2005.

[132] Statement of William J. Fox, director, Financial Crimes Enforcement Network, U.S. Department of the Treasury, before the Senate Committee on Banking, Housing, and Urban Affairs, September 28, 2004.

[133] Racinos are racetracks with electronic gaming devices. The term "racino" has not been separately defined nor included specifically in the definition of casino for purposes of the BSA.  Instead, FinCEN has relied on the state, territory or tribal characterization of "racino"gaming in determining whether an entity or operation should be treated as a casino for purposes of the BSA.  Therefore, if state law defines or characterizes slot machine operations at a racetrack as a "casino, gambling casino, or gaming establishment," and the gross annual gaming revenues of that operation exceed the $1 million threshold, then the operation would be deemed to be a "casino" for purposes of the BSA and subject to all applicable requirements.

[134] The InfoShop, Report: Casino Gambling—U.S. (Nov. 2004). Accessed at:  http://www.the-infoshop.com/study/mt25476_casino_gambling.html.

[135] National Indian Gaming Association, An Analysis of the Economic Impact of Indian Gaming in 2004. Accessed at: http://www.indiangaming.org.

[136] MSNBC, Tribal Casino Revenues Double Nevada's, Feb. 15, 2005.  Accessed at: http://www.msnbc.msn.com/id/6976517/.

Mashantucket Pequot Tribe. The west coast (primarily California) represents the fastest growing region for the Indian gaming industry.[137]

According to FinCEN, most tribal casinos are small to mid-size operations typically without deposit or credit accounts for customers and with few gaming tables, relying instead on slot machines for gaming revenues. Commercial casinos, by comparison, offer more table games. Table games require more cash handling on the gaming floor than slot machines. Consequently, commercial casinos offer more sophisticated account services and, correspondingly, pose a greater money laundering threat.[138]

## Vulnerabilities

Law enforcement and media reports indicate that criminals typically launder money through casinos by exchanging illicit cash for casino chips and then either:

- Holding the chips for a period of time and later cashing them in for a casino check or having the casino wire the money elsewhere;

- Using the chips as currency to purchase narcotics, with the drug dealer later cashing in the chips; or,

- Using the chips to gamble in hopes of generating certifiable winnings.

Criminals also use casinos to launder counterfeit money as well as large currency notes that would be conspicuous and difficult to use elsewhere, and which may be marked by undercover law enforcement officers. Suspicious activities at casinos often involve customers structuring transactions to avoid recordkeeping or reporting thresholds, using agents to cash-out multiple transactions for an anonymous individual, providing false documents or identifying information, or layering transactions to disguise their source.

The IRS-Criminal Investigation division reports the following case examples of casinos used for money laundering:

- Criminals laundered money through video poker games by feeding illicit proceeds into the machines (one, five, and ten dollar bills) and then either after playing briefly or not at all, they pressed the "cash out" button which generated a receipt that was redeemed for a casino check.

- A major cocaine and heroin dealer played the $100 slot machines in Las Vegas and Atlantic City, wagering hundreds of thousands of dollars, in order to receive a casino check for his eventual winnings and an IRS Form W-2G to legitimize the income. The drug dealer also purchased Pennsylvania lottery tickets from winners, paying them more than the winning payout in order to receive a state check and an IRS Form W-2. The individual eventually invested the laundered money in rental properties.

- While criminals will often structure their transactions to avoid financial institutions' filing CTRs, money launderers using casinos have the opposite strategy. In one case, a number of people purchased chips with illicit cash in amounts below the CTR threshold, but then passed the chips to one individual who cashed out, receiving a casino check and triggering the filing of a CTR that gave the appearance of further authenticating the transaction. Over a twelve-month period, one individual was named in casino CTRs reporting $1.1 million paid out, but was not named in a single CTR for cash taken in.

- In one case, a money launderer purchased casino rewards cards from legitimate patrons. The cards increase in value with each casino visit and with each gambling session. The cards were purchased with illicit cash and were then traded in for gold coins at a casino store. An employee at the store was an accomplice in the laundering scheme.

A constant threat at casinos is insiders taking advantage of their position either to steal or assist others with money laundering. ICE recently charged six people, in-

---

[137] *Ibid.*

[138] Many offer front money (deposit and withdrawal) accounts where money is deposited by a customer into a casino account at the cage that the customer can later withdraw at either the cage (in the form of casino check, currency, money transfer, etc.) or at the gaming tables (in the form of chips to bet or wager with).

cluding a tribal leader, with attempting to steal $900,000 from a Native American casino. Among the charges are conspiracy, theft, and money laundering.

## Regulation and Public Policy

Casinos in the United States are subject to a decentralized regulatory structure and are primarily regulated by the states and by tribal regulatory authorities. Under the BSA and its implementing regulations, a gaming operation is defined as a financial institution subject to the requirements of the BSA if it has annual gaming revenue of more than $1,000,000 and is licensed as a gaming establishment under state or local law and authorized to do business in the United States, or is an Indian gaming operation conducted under or pursuant to the Indian Gaming Regulatory Act (IGRA).[139]

State-licensed gambling casinos were generally made subject to the recordkeeping and currency reporting requirements of the BSA by regulation in 1985. Casinos authorized to do business under the IGRA[140] were made subject to the BSA in 1996. Card clubs became subject to the BSA in 1998.

Casinos in Nevada, with gross annual gaming revenues of $10,000,000 or more and "table games statistical win" of $2 million or more, currently are, under a special agreement with the Department of the Treasury, subject to Nevada Gaming Commission Regulation 6A. The Nevada Gaming Commission's regulation, like the BSA, stipulates currency reporting and recordkeeping requirements.[141]

All casinos (including those in Nevada) and card clubs, with gross annual gaming revenue in excess of $1,000,000, are required to file casino CTRs to report each currency transaction involving cash-in or cash-out of more than $10,000 in a "gaming day" with a customer. Under the BSA, multiple currency transactions conducted by or on behalf of the same customer on the same gaming day are considered to be one transaction for CTR purposes.

In September 2002, FinCEN adopted a rule requiring casinos (including those in Nevada) and card clubs to file SARs for suspicious transactions occurring after March 25, 2003. SARs must be filed for any suspicious transaction that involves or aggregates at least $5,000 in funds or other assets. Nevada casinos with gross annual gaming revenue of $1,000,000 or more are subject to BSA requirements to (i) establish and maintain a written anti-money laundering program and (ii) report suspicious activity.[142] Further, Nevada casinos that are not subject to Regulation 6A, but that have gross annual gaming revenue in excess of $1,000,000, are subject to all of the provisions of the BSA applicable to casinos generally.[143] FinCEN has delegated authority to the IRS to examine Nevada casinos for compliance with the BSA.

Since April of 1999, FinCEN has brought a number of enforcement actions against casinos for BSA violations.[144] In an effort to head off a large-scale failure on the part of a casino to file the required BSA forms, FinCEN has developed with the IRS an "early warning system." It involves a monthly database query comparing the volume of casino CTRs filed for the current month with the volume of CTRs filed during the same month the previous year. The database query produces a report listing casinos whose CTR filing volume has fallen by 30 percent or more. The hope is that this early warning system will flag a casino that is substantially disregarding its BSA obligations.

---

[139]  *See* 31 U.S.C. § 5312(a)(2)(X) and 31 C.F.R. §§ 103.11(n)(5)(i) and (n)(6)(i).

[140]  The Indian Gaming Regulatory Act, Section 1 of Pub. L. 100-497 (1988) (codified generally at 25 U.S.C. § 2701 et seq.), established the jurisdictional framework that governs Indian gaming. The Act establishes three classes of games with a different regulatory scheme for each. Class I gaming is defined as traditional Indian gaming and social gaming for minimal prizes. Regulatory authority over class I gaming is vested exclusively in tribal governments. Class II gaming is basically bingo operations, and although primarily regulated by the Tribes, they must comply with National Indian Gaming Commission's Minimal Internal Control Standards. Class III gaming is comparable to casino gaming and is subject to BSA requirements as well as National Indian Gaming Commission requirements.

[141]  The Nevada Gaming Control Board recommended the repeal of Regulation 6A to the Nevada Gaming Commission at the Commission's May 19, 2005 meeting. In the meantime, FinCEN is developing an information sharing Memorandum of Understanding to be entered into with the Board to assure consistency in the application of Bank Secrecy Act requirements. FinCEN also will be working with the Board and the IRS to assure consistency in examining Nevada casinos for Bank Secrecy Act compliance.

[142]  *See* 31 C.F.R. §§ 103.64(a), 103.120(d), and 103.21.

[143]  *See* 31 C.F.R. § 103.

[144]  *See* FinCEN, Regulatory/Enforcement Actions. Accessed at: http://www.fincen.gov/reg_enforcement.html.

Part of the challenge of establishing an effective BSA oversight regime for tribal casinos is coordinating the various regulatory bodies. Tribal governmental gaming is regulated on three levels:

- Tribes regulate their own gaming operations through tribal gaming commissions, compliance officers, tribal law enforcement officers, and tribal courts.

- States regulate tribal gaming at a level negotiated through tribal/state compacts.

- The federal government regulates tribal gaming through:

    1. The National Indian Gaming Commission, which is the primary federal regulator, providing oversight, reviewing licensing of gaming management and key employees, management contracts, and tribal gaming ordinances;

    2. The Secretary of the Interior, who oversees the Tribal-State compact process, and reviews and approves compacts;

    3. The Department of the Treasury which, through FinCEN, implements the BSA as it applies to tribal casino operations; and,

    4. The Department of Justice, which, through the FBI, has federal criminal jurisdiction over acts directly related to Indian gaming establishments.

The IGRA gives the FBI federal criminal jurisdiction over acts directly related to Indian gaming, including those located on reservations under state criminal jurisdiction. The FBI's Indian Country Unit established the Indian Gaming Working Group (IGWG) in February 2003 to identify and direct resources to Indian gaming matters and to focus on "national impact" cases.[145] However, the FBI acknowledges that it has been able to devote limited investigative resources to Indian gaming violations even as the Indian gaming industry has grown. This growth, coupled with overlapping regulatory jurisdictions and limited enforcement resources, has generated concern over the potential for large-scale criminal activity in the Indian gaming industry.

---

[145] IGWG members include FinCEN, the FBI, the Department of Interior-Office of Inspector General, the National Indian Gaming Commission, the Internal Revenue Service Tribal Government Section, the U.S. Department of Justice, and the Bureau of Indian Affairs.

## Suspicious Activity Report

by Casinos & Card Clubs (SAR–C) Filings by Type of Gaming Establishment August 1, 1996 through December 31, 2004

| Type of Gaming Establishment | 1996 | 1997 | 1998 | 1999 | 2000 | 2001 | 2002 | 2003 | 2004 |
|---|---|---|---|---|---|---|---|---|---|
| State Licensed Casino | – | 22 | 288 | 262 | 309 | 1,215 | 1,621 | 4,393 | 4,694 |
| Tribal Licensed Casino | – | 21 | 117 | 112 | 115 | 114 | 120 | 539 | 936 |
| Card Club | – | – | 3 | 3 | 1 | 1 | 9 | 19 | 27 |
| Other | – | – | – | 3 | – | – | – | 1 | 1 |
| Unspecific/Blank | 85 | 2 | 152 | 70 | 45 | 48 | 84 | 165 | 121 |
| Unspecific/Blank | 85 | 2 | 152 | 70 | 45 | 48 | 84 | 165 | 121 |

Source: Financial Crimes Enforcement Network

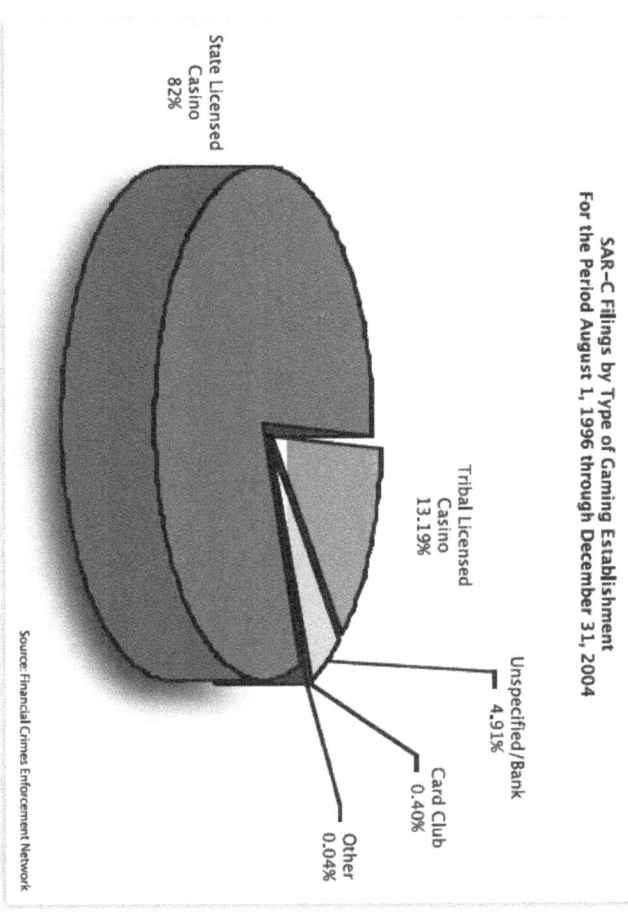

State Licensed Casino
82%

Tribal Licensed Casino
13.19%

Unspecified/Bank
4.91%

Card Club
0.40%

Other
0.04%

**SAR–C Filings by Type of Gaming Establishment
For the Period August 1, 1996 through December 31, 2004**

Source: Financial Crimes Enforcement Network

Table 11

## Appendix A
# NDIC ANALYSIS

As part of the 2005 Money Laundering Threat Assessment, the National Drug Intelligence Center (NDIC) analyzed asset seizure data from five federal law enforcement agencies (CBP, DEA, FBI, ICE, and IRS-CI) to identify the top cities for asset seizures in the United States. NDIC analysts compared all available asset seizure data from 2001-2004, to reduce biases that arise from anomalous years.

The analysis was hindered by certain incompatibilities among the data sets, most significantly variations in the geographic boundaries among agency districts and variations in the types of assets counted by the respective agencies (cash and monetary instruments only vs. all seized property). NDIC harmonized the geographic disparities by shifting their focus to primary metropolitan centers and performing a county-by-county comparison of regional overlaps among agency districts to ensure that similar regions were being compared.

To minimize distortions caused by differences in individual agencies' systems of collecting data, NDIC began by assembling separate rankings of the top seizure regions for each agency independently. A score of "1" was assigned to the region with the highest seizure total, and so on. Each agency's scores were then weighted based on that agency's aggregate seizure figures as a proportion of total U.S. seizures. All agencies' weighted scores were totaled to derive, for each region, an aggregate, inter-agency score. (See Table 12) As a check, NDIC also tallied the original, unweighted rankings, thereby assigning each law enforcement agency's scores equal weight. The outcome was identical for the top five cities, with minor changes among the bottom, closely-spaced five.[146]

Notably, there is a substantial gap between the amounts of money laundering being detected in the top three regions and the rest of the country. As one proceeds beyond the top few regions, the incremental differences in seizure totals and scores shrink dramatically.

To corroborate the validity of these rankings, NDIC overlaid data from FinCEN and from the DEA's Federal Drug Seizure System (FDSS).[147] Using the locations of the police organizations filing information requests through FinCEN under Section 314(a) of the USA PATRIOT Act, NDIC was able to determine that approximately 81% of the criminal cases underlying the 314(a) requests were in the top ten cities for asset seizures and

Table 12

| Region | Score | Ranking |
|--------|-------|---------|
| New York | 1.92 | 1 |
| Miami | 3.40 | 2 |
| Los Angeles | 3.74 | 3 |
| Phoenix/Tucson | 6.61 | 4 |
| Houston | 8.12 | 5 |
| Boston | 8.50 | 6 |
| Detroit | 8.52 | 7 |
| San Juan | 8.55 | 8 |
| Atlanta | 8.60 | 9 |
| Chicago | 8.85 | 10 |

61% of the cases were in the top three cities. That finding accords with the fact that, in the law enforcement data sets NDIC used, the total dollar amount seized in the top three cities (New York, Miami, and Los Angeles) exceeded the total dollar amount seized in the rest of the top ten cities combined.

Data from FDSS, which tallies federal law enforcement drug seizures, also revealed a close correlation with the top ranked cities for asset seizures. (See Table 13)

---

[146] The unweighted order of the cities was (1) New York; (2) Miami; (3) Los Angeles; (4) Phoenix/Tucson; (5) Houston; (6) Detroit; (7) Chicago; (8) Atlanta; (9) Boston; (10) San Juan.

[147] *Federal-Wide Drug Seizures: Drug Seizures Ranked By Top Five Areas*, Drug Intelligence Brief, Drug Enforcement Administration, Intelligence Division, DEA 04026, June 2004.

Indeed, NDIC's analysis suggests that drug money may be the most common source of illicit proceeds being laundered in the United States. It should be noted, however, that there is not full overlap between the asset seizure top ten cities list and the top ten drug markets in the country,[148] and other criminal activity – such as fraud and white collar crime – is represented in the asset seizure figures in significant numbers.

Table 13

| Ranking of States Based on Federal Drug Seizure System data (1999–2003) | | | | | | | |
|---|---|---|---|---|---|---|---|
| Heroin | | Cocaine | | Marijuana | | Methamphetamine | |
| NY | 1 | TX | 1 | TX | 1 | CA | 1 |
| FL | 2 | FL | 2 | AR | 2 | TX | 2 |
| CA | 3 | CA | 3 | CA | 3 | AR | 3 |
| TX | 4 | PR | 4 | NM | 4 | FL | 4 |
| NJ | 5 | NY | 5 | FL | 5 | GA | 5 |
| PR | 6 | | | PR | 6 | NM | 6 |

Source: Federal Drug Seizure System

## Appendix B
# FinCEN ANALYSIS

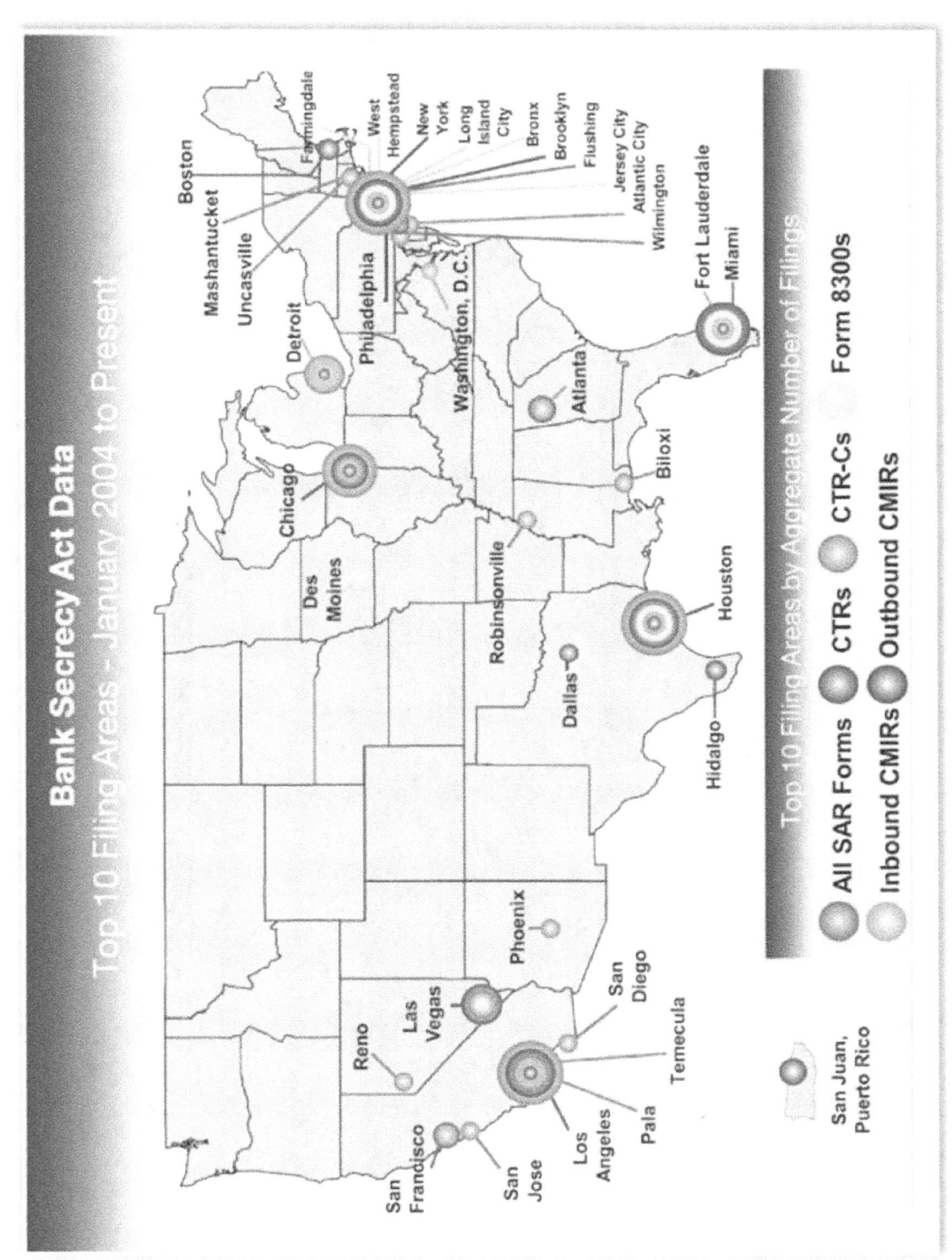

**Bank Secrecy Act Data**
Top 10 Filing Areas – January 2004 to Present

Top 10 Filing Areas by Aggregate Number of Filings

- All SAR Forms
- CTRs
- CTR-Cs
- Form 8300s
- Inbound CMIRs
- Outbound CMIRs

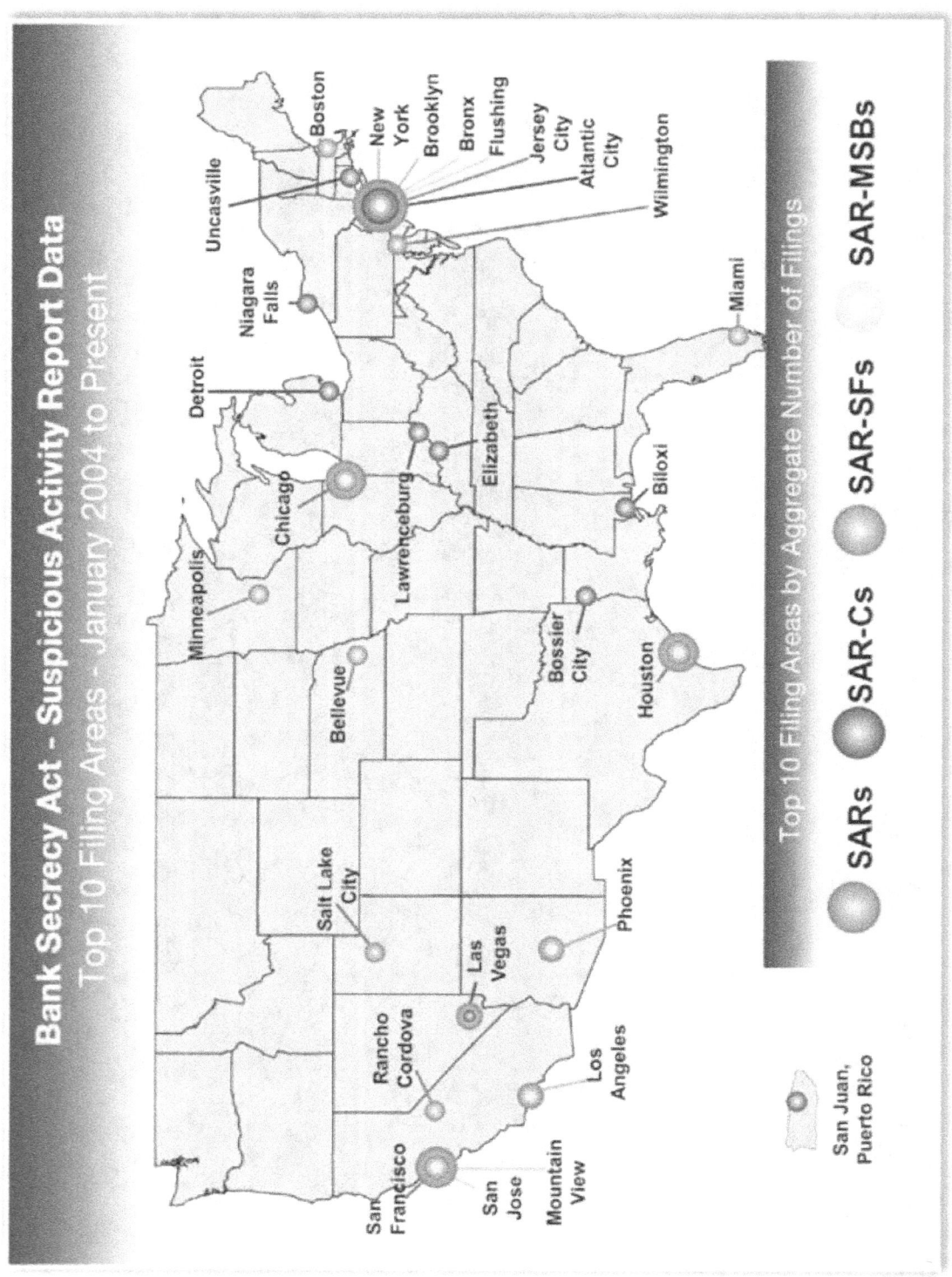

**Bank Secrecy Act - Suspicious Activity Report Data**
Top 10 Filing Areas - January 2004 to Present

Top 10 Filing Areas by Aggregate Number of Filings

SARs    SAR-Cs    SAR-SFs    SAR-MSBs

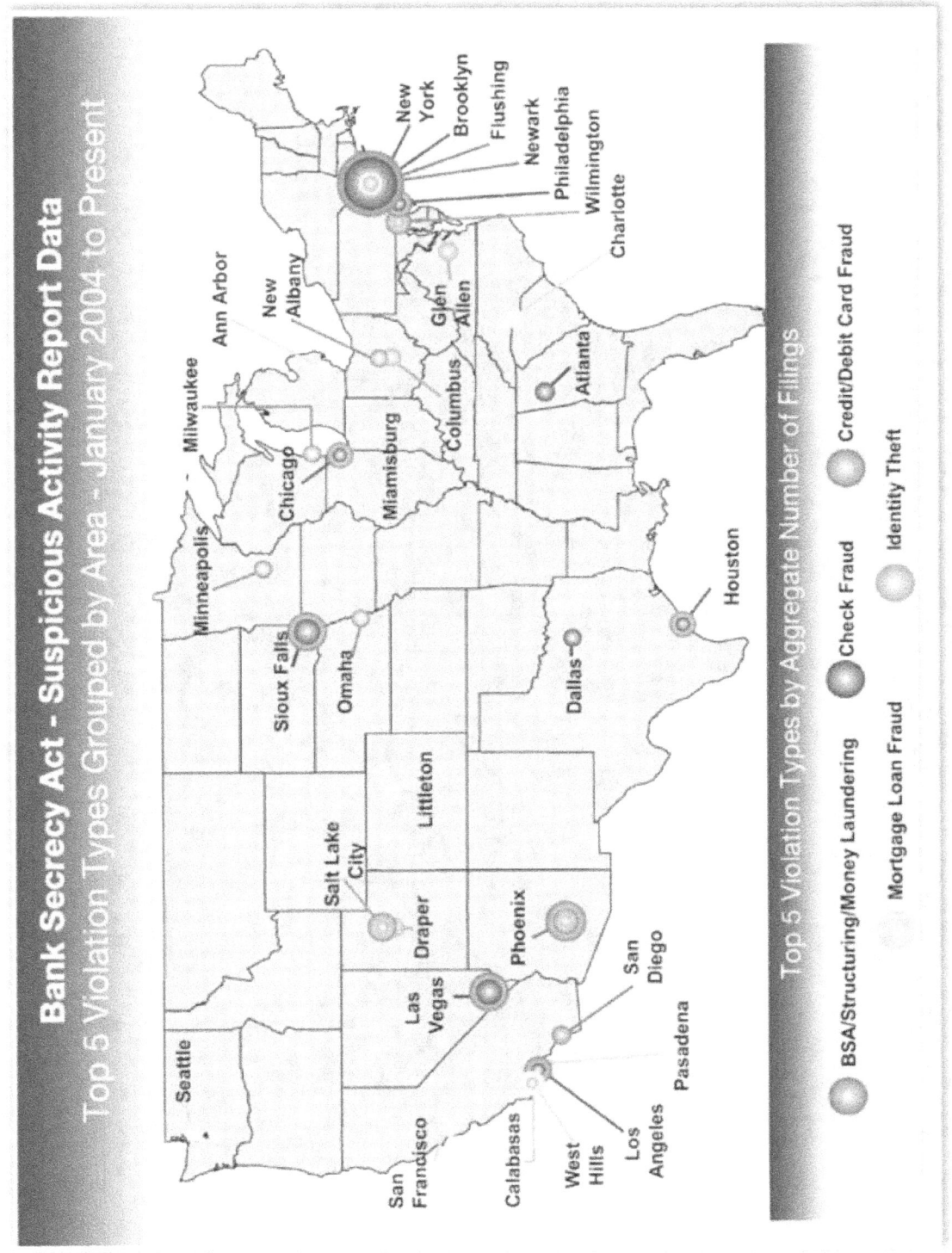

**Bank Secrecy Act - Suspicious Activity Report Data**
Top 5 Violation Types Grouped by Area – January 2004 to Present

Top 5 Violation Types by Aggregate Number of Filings

BSA/Structuring/Money Laundering
Mortgage Loan Fraud
Check Fraud
Credit/Debit Card Fraud
Identity Theft

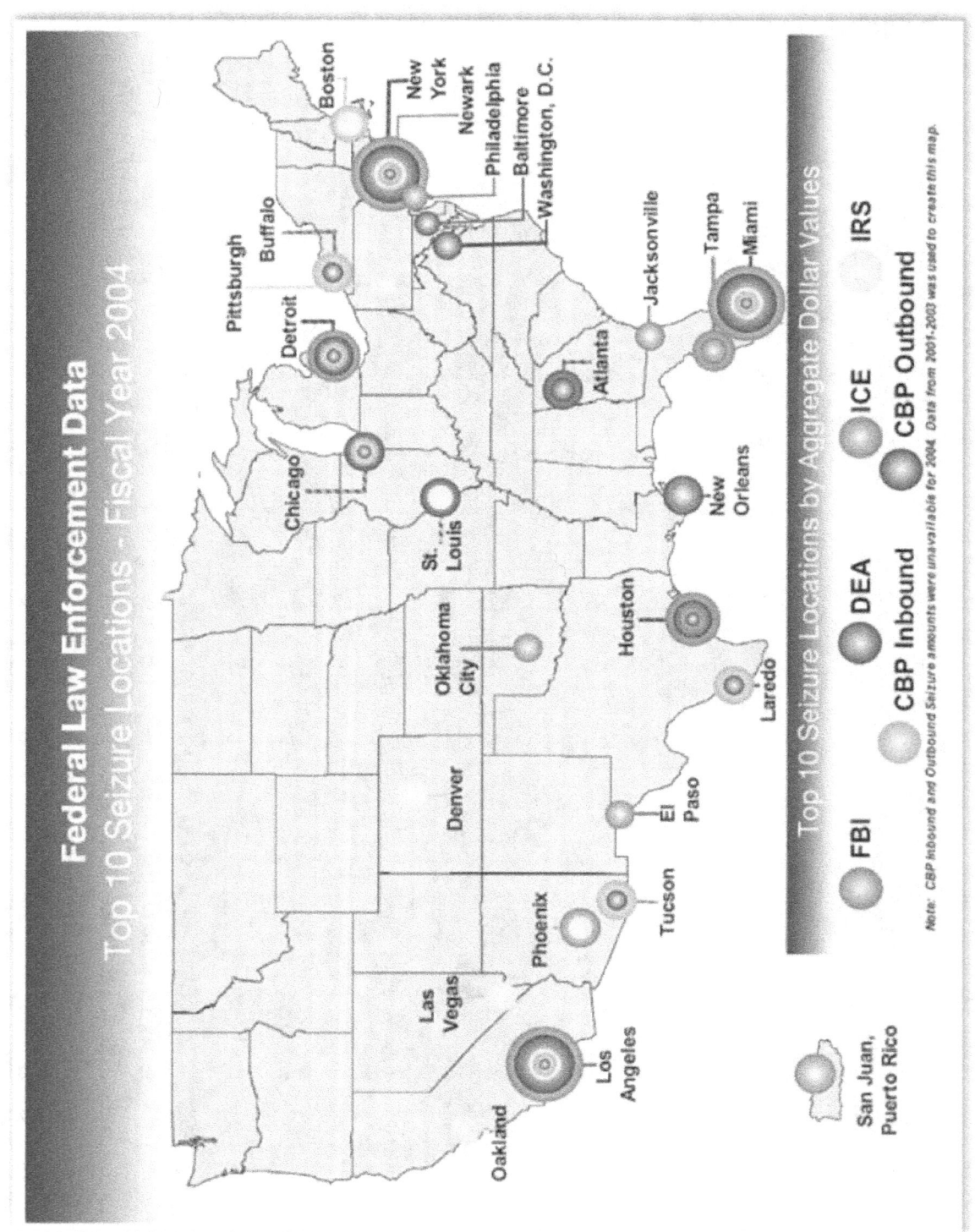

Federal Law Enforcement Data
Top 10 Seizure Locations – Fiscal Year 2004

Top 10 Seizure Locations by Aggregate Dollar Values

FBI    DEA    ICE    IRS

CBP Inbound    CBP Outbound

Note: CBP Inbound and Outbound Seizure amounts were unavailable for 2004. Data from 2001-2003 was used to create this map.

## Top Ten Suspicious Activity Report Filing Locations January 2004 to Present

### Depository Institution SARs

| Filer City | Count |
| --- | --- |
| New York, NY | 28,187 |
| Los Angeles, CA | 19,379 |
| Wilmington, DE | 11,796 |
| Phoenix, AZ | 11,329 |
| Houston, TX | 10,444 |
| Salt Lake City, UT | 8,757 |
| San Francisco, CA | 8,633 |
| Chicago, IL | 7,385 |
| Las Vegas, NV | 7,223 |
| Brooklyn, NY | 7,005 |

### SAR-Cs

| Filer City | Count |
| --- | --- |
| Atlantic City, NJ | 2,796 |
| Las Vegas, NV | 984 |
| Biloxi, MS | 441 |
| Uncasville, CT | 270 |
| Bossier City, LA | 262 |
| Detroit, MI | 259 |
| Lawrenceburg, IN | 196 |
| Elizabeth, IN | 144 |
| Niagara Falls, NY | 142 |
| San Juan, PR | 136 |

### SAR-MSBs

| Filer City | Count |
| --- | --- |
| New York, NY | 21,259 |
| Phoenix, AZ | 14,678 |
| Houston, TX | 14,071 |
| Los Angeles, CA | 12,538 |
| Flushing, NY | 11,717 |
| Brooklyn, NY | 10,025 |
| Mountain View, CA | 9,160 |
| San Jose, CA | 8,458 |
| Chicago, IL | 7,236 |
| Bronx, NY | 7,140 |

### SAR-SFs

| Filer City | Count |
| --- | --- |
| New York, NY | 1,161 |
| Bellevue, | 986 |
| Boston, MA | 698 |
| Minneapolis, MN | 458 |
| San Francisco, CA | 456 |
| Rancho Cordova, CA | 441 |
| Chicago, IL | 230 |
| Jersey City, NJ | 207 |
| Miami, FL | 117 |
| Houston, TX | 103 |

## Top Ten Suspicious Activity Report Filing Locations January 2004 to Present (Continued)

### Top Ten Suspicious Activity Report (All SAR Forms) Filing Locations January 2004 to Present

| Filer City | Count |
|---|---|
| New York, NY | 50,607 |
| Los Angeles, CA | 31,917 |
| Phoenix, AZ | 26,007 |
| Houston, TX | 24,618 |
| Brooklyn, NY | 17,101 |
| Flushing, NY | 15,789 |
| Chicago, IL | 14,851 |
| Wilmington, DE | 11,796 |
| San Jose, CA | 11,362 |
| San Diego, CA | 9,168 |

### Top Ten Currency Transaction Report Filing Locations January 2004 to Present

| Filer City | Count |
|---|---|
| Los Angeles, CA | 471,583 |
| New York, NY | 352,183 |
| Chicago, IL | 336,530 |
| Houston, TX | 281,943 |
| Las Vegas, NV | 198,274 |
| Miami, FL | 195,326 |
| Brooklyn, NY | 185,960 |
| Dallas, TX | 154,639 |
| Philadelphia, PA | 138,755 |
| San Francisco, CA | 138,217 |

### Top Ten Currency Transaction Report by Casino Filing Locations January 2004 to Present

| Casino City | Count |
|---|---|
| Las Vegas, NV | 190,358 |
| Atlantic City, NJ | 93,280 |
| Uncasville, CT | 26,072 |
| Biloxi, MS | 22,951 |
| Mashantucket, CT | 17,098 |
| Robinsonville, MS | 16,721 |
| Reno, NV | 16,153 |
| Detroit, MI | 15,269 |
| Temecula, CA | 12,778 |
| Pala, CA | 10,857 |

### Top Ten Form 8300 Filing Locations January 2004 to Present

| Business Location | Count |
|---|---|
| West Hempstead, NY | 7,783 |
| Miami, FL | 7,468 |
| New York, NY | 5,930 |
| Long Island City, NY | 3,889 |
| Jersey City, NJ | 3,254 |
| Houston, TX | 2,921 |
| Bronx, NY | 2,749 |
| Farmingdale, NY | 2,691 |
| Las Vegas, NV | 2,384 |
| Des Moines, IA | 2,255 |

## Top Ten Suspicious Activity Report Filing Locations January 2004 to Present (Continued)

| Top Ten Outbound CMIR Filing Locations January 2004 to Present | | Top Ten Inbound CMIR Filing Locations January 2004 to Present | |
|---|---|---|---|
| Exported From City | Count | Imported To City | Count |
| New York, NY | 4,255 | Miami, FL | 36,869 |
| Los Angeles, CA | 4,059 | Los Angeles, CA | 27,157 |
| Miami, FL | 3,354 | New York, NY | 10,119 |
| Chicago, IL | 1,911 | San Francisco, CA | 8,675 |
| Atlanta, GA | 1,901 | Chicago, IL | 5,970 |
| Detroit, MI | 1,868 | Atlanta, GA | 5,014 |
| Hidalgo, TX | 1,624 | Houston, TX | 4,663 |
| Boston, MA | 999 | Detroit, MI | 4,047 |
| Houston, TX | 944 | Fort Lauderdale, FL | 3,909 |
| San Juan, PR | 815 | Washington, DC | 3,833 |

| Top Five Suspicious Activity Report (All SAR Forms) Violation Types Grouped by Area January 2004 to Present | | | | | |
| --- | --- | --- | --- | --- | --- |
| BSA/Structuring/ Money Laundering | | Check Fraud[149] | | Credit/Debit Card Fraud[150] | |
| Filer City | Count | Filer City | Count | Filer City | Count |
| New York, NY | 60,802 | Sioux Falls, SD | 1,901 | Phoenix, AZ | 7,784 |
| Los Angeles, CA | 32,747 | Chicago, IL | 1,556 | Wilmington, DE | 4,870 |
| Flushing, NY | 30,768 | New York, NY | 1,477 | Salt Lake City, UT | 4,185 |
| Houston, TX | 23,258 | Los Angeles, CA | 948 | Sioux Falls, SD | 2,962 |
| Phoenix, AZ | 20,066 | Houston, TX | 695 | New York, NY | 1,862 |
| Brooklyn, NY | 18,294 | Brooklyn, NY | 549 | Las Vegas, NV | 1,281 |
| Chicago, IL | 10,307 | Philadelphia, PA | 515 | Minneapolis, MN | 1,184 |
| Philadelphia, PA | 9,845 | Atlanta, GA | 500 | Milwaukee, WI | 871 |
| San Diego, CA | 9,224 | Las Vegas, NV | 476 | Omaha, NE | 741 |
| Newark, NJ | 9,018 | Dallas, TX | 465 | New Albany, OH | 726 |

[149] The violation type "Check Fraud" does not occur on the Money Services Business SAR form.
[150] The violation type "Credit/Debit Card Fraud" does not occur on the Money Services Business SAR form.

## Top Five Suspicious Activity Report
## (All SAR Forms) Violation Types Grouped by Area
## January 2004 to Present (Continued)

| Mortgage Loan Fraud[151] | | Identity Theft[152] | |
|---|---|---|---|
| Filer City | DCN Count | Filer City | DCN Count |
| Ann Arbor, MI | 3,225 | Wilmington, DE | 8,670 |
| San Francisco, CA | 2,567 | Salt Lake City, UT | 5,512 |
| Seattle, WA | 2,346 | Phoenix, AZ | 5,191 |
| Calabasas, CA | 1,710 | Sioux Falls, SD | 3,400 |
| New York, NY | 1,331 | Las Vegas, NV | 1,746 |
| Pasadena, CA | 1,302 | New York, NY | 1,229 |
| Miamisburg, OH | 1,172 | Draper, UT | 801 |
| West Hills, CA | 1,000 | Calabasas, CA | 608 |
| Littleton, CO | 796 | Glen Allen, VA | 442 |
| Charlotte, NC | 750 | Columbus, OH | 411 |

---

[151] The violation type "Mortgage Loan Fraud" only occurs on the Depository Institution SAR form. BSA data relating to "Mortgage Loan fraud" only pertains to those SARs filed by Depository Institutions.

[152] The violation type "Identity Theft" only occurs on the Depository Institution SAR form and the Securities and Futures Industries SAR form. BSA data relating to "Identity Theft" only pertains to those SARs filed by Depository Institutions and the Securities and Futures

Appendix C
# BANK SECRECY ACT REPORTS

| Report | Requirements | Filed in CY 2004 |
|---|---|---|
| Currency Transaction Report (CTR) | Filed by financial institutions that engage in a currency transaction in excess of $10,000 | 13,115,305 |
| Currency Transaction Report Casino (CTRC) | Filed by a casino to report currency transactions in excess of $10,000. | 483,740 |
| Report of Foreign Bank and Financial Accounts (FBAR) | Filed by individuals to report a financial interest in or signatory authority over one or more accounts in foreign countries, if the aggregate value of these accounts exceeds $10,000 at any time during the calendar year. | 219,105 |
| IRS Form 8300, Report of Cash Payments Over $10,000 Received in a Trade or Business | Filed by persons engaged in a trade or business who, in the course of that trade or business, receives more than $10,000 in cash in one transaction or two or more related transactions within a twelve month period. | 152,683 |
| Suspicious Activity Report (SAR) | Filed by depository institutions on transactions or attempted transactions involving at least $5,000 that the financial institution knows, suspects, or has reason to suspect: <ul><li>involve money derived from illegal activities;</li><li>are intended or conducted in order to hide or disguise funds or assets derived from illegal activity;</li><li>are designed to evade BSA requirements or other financial reporting requirements (structuring); or</li><li>have no business or apparent lawful purpose.</li></ul> | 381,671 |
| Suspicious Activity Report Casino (SARC) | Filed on transactions or attempted transactions conducted or attempted by, at, or through a casino/card club, and involving or aggregating at least $5,000 in funds or other assets, and the casino/card club knows, suspects, or has reason to suspect that the transactions or pattern of transactions: <ul><li>involve money derived from illegal activities;</li><li>are intended or conducted in order to hide or disguise funds or assets derived from illegal activity;</li><li>are designed to evade BSA requirements or other financial reporting requirements (structuring);</li><li>have no business or apparent lawful purpose; or</li><li>involve the use of the casino/card club to facilitate criminal activity.</li></ul> | 5,754 |
| Report of International Transportation of Currency or Monetary Instruments (CMIR) | Filed by individuals or businesses who transport, or cause the transportation of, $10,000 or more in currency or other negotiable instruments into or out of the United States. | 149,956 |

| Report | Requirements | Filed in CY 2004 |
|---|---|---|
| Registration of Money Services Business | Each money services business (MSB) must register except for (1) one that is a money services business solely because it serves as an agent of another MSB, (2) the U.S. Postal Service, and (3) issuers, sellers, and redeemers of stored value. | 10,254 |
| Suspicious Activity Report by Money Services Businesses (SAR–MSB) | Filed on transactions or attempted transactions conducted or attempted by, at, or through an MSB, and involving or aggregating funds or other assets of at least $2,000 in funds or other assets, and the MSB knows, suspects, or has reason to suspect that the transactions or pattern of transactions:<br><br>• involve money derived from illegal activities;<br><br>• are intended or conducted in order to hide or disguise funds or assets derived from illegal activity;;<br><br>• are designed to evade BSA requirements or other financial reporting requirements (structuring);<br><br>• have no business or apparent lawful purpose; or<br><br>• involve the use of the MSB to facilitate criminal activity.<br>When transactions are identified from a review of records of money orders or traveler's checks that have been sold or processed, an issuer of money orders of traveler's checks shall be required to report a transaction or a pattern of transactions that involves or aggregates funds or other assets of at least $5,000. | 296,284 |
| Suspicious Activity Report by the Securities & Futures Industries (SAR-SF) | Filed on transactions, or attempted transactions, if it is conducted by, at, or through a broker–dealer, a futures commission merchant (FCM), or an introducing broker in commodities (IB–C) and it involves or aggregates funds or other assets of at least $5,000, and the broker–dealer/FCM/IB–C knows, suspects, or has reason to suspect that the transaction involves funds derived from illegal activities, is intended or conducted in order to hide or disguise funds or assets derived from illegal activity, is designed to evade BSA requirements (structuring), has no business or apparent lawful purpose, or involves use of the broker–dealer/FCM/IB–C to facilitate criminal activity. Also filed when transactions are designed, whether through structuring or other means, to evade filing requirements. Also filed when a transaction has no business or apparent lawful purpose or is not the sort in which the particular customer would normally be expected to engage, and the broker–dealer knows of no reasonable explanation for the transaction after examining the available facts. Also filed when the transaction involves the use of the broker–dealer to facilitate criminal activity. | 5,705 |
| Designation of Exempt Person | Used by bank or other depository institution to designate an eligible customer as an exempt person from currency transaction reporting rules. | 67,935 |

Source: FinCEN

## Appendix D
# STATUS OF BSA REGULATIONS FOR FINANCIAL INSTITUTIONS

| Type of Institution | Subject to the BSA Rules (Other than Form 8300) | Requirements | Must have an AML Program | Must file SARs | Must file CTR's | Must file 8300s | Must have a Customer Identification Program (CIP) |
|---|---|---|---|---|---|---|---|
| MSBs[153] | Yes | Title 31 CFR § § [103.11, 20, 22, 23, 24, 25, 27, 28, 29, 33, 37, 41, and 125] | Yes | Yes[154] | Yes | No | No |
| Banks | Yes | Title 31 CFR § § [103.11, 18, 22, 23, 24, 25, 26, 27, 28, 33, 120, 177, 181 and 183] | Yes | Yes | Yes | No | Yes |
| Insurance Companies | Currently exempt under 31 CFR § 103.170. | Proposed AML and SAR Rules are at 68 FR 8480 (Feb. 21, 2003] and 67 FR 64067 (Oct. 17, 2002). Final AML and SAR Rules in preparation. | No | No | No | Yes | No |
| Securities Broker–Dealers | Yes | Title 31 CFR § § [103.11, 19, 23, 24, 35, 120 and 122] | Yes | Yes | Yes | No | Yes |
| Travel Agencies | Currently exempt under 31 CFR § 103.170. | An ANPRM[155] was issued on February 24, 2003. | No | No | No | Yes | No |
| Investment Advisers | Currently exempt under 31 CFR § 103.170 | Proposed AML Rule at 68 FR 23640 (May 5, 2003). | No | No | No | Yes | No |
| Pawn Brokers | Currently exempt under 31 CFR § 103.170. | Proposed rules in preparation. | No | No | No | Yes | No |
| Futures Commission Merchants and Introducing Brokers–Commodities | Yes | Title 31 CFR § § [103.11, 17, 22, 23, 24, 27, 120 and 123]. | Yes | Yes | Yes | No | Yes |

Table title: A QUICK GUIDE TO THE STATUS OF BANK SECRECY ACT (BSA) / USA PATRIOT ACT REGULATIONS FOR FINANCIAL INSTITUTIONS IN THE U.S (as of August 2005)

[153] The following are defined as MSBs: check cashers who conduct transactions in amounts over $1,000 per person per day, currency dealers or exchangers who conduct transactions in amounts over $1,000 per person per day, issuers of traveler's checks, money orders and stored value who conduct transactions in amounts over $1,000 per person per day, sellers or redeemers of traveler's checks, money orders or stored value who conduct transactions in amounts over $1,000 per person per day, money transmitters, and USPS.

[154] Only certain MSBs must file SARs. These include money transmitters, currency dealers or exchangers, money order - issuers, sellers, or redeemers, traveler's check-issuers, sellers, or redeemers, and USPS.

[155] Advanced Notice of Proposed Rulemaking (ANPRM) is a means to seek comment and specific data from stakeholders and the public on important complex or controversial issues prior to issuance of a notice of proposed rulemaking. No regulatory text is required.

### A QUICK GUIDE TO THE STATUS OF BANK SECRECY ACT (BSA) / USA PATRIOT ACT REGULATIONS FOR FINANCIAL INSTITUTIONS IN THE U.S (as of August 2005)

| Type of Institution | Subject to the BSA Rules (Other than Form 8300) | Requirements | Must have an AML Program | Must file SARs | Must file CTR's | Must file 8300s | Must have a Customer Identification Program (CIP) |
|---|---|---|---|---|---|---|---|
| Unregistered Investment Companies | Currently exempt under 31 CFR § 103.170. | Proposed AML Rule at 67 Fed. Reg. 60617 (Sept. 26, 2002) | No | No | No | Yes | No |
| Mutual Funds | Yes | Title 31 CFR § § 103. 23, 24, 130 and 131 Proposed SAR Rule at 68 Fed. Reg. 2716 (Jan. 21, 2003). | Yes | No | No | Yes | Yes |
| Loan and Finance Companies | Currently exempt under 31 CFR § 103.170. | Proposed rules in preparation. | No | No | No | Yes | No |
| Dealers in Precious Metals, Stones or Jewels | Yes | 31 CFR § 103.23, 24, 140 | Yes | No | No | Yes | No |
| Credit Card System Operators | Yes | 31 CFR § 103.135 | Yes | No | No | Yes | No |
| Businesses Engaged in Vehicle Sales | Currently exempt under 31 CFR § 103.170. | An ANPRM was issued at 68 FR 8568 (Feb. 24, 2003). | No | No | No | Yes | No |
| Casinos | Yes | Title 31 CFR § § [103.11, 21, 22, 23, 24, 36 and 120]. | Yes | Yes | Yes | No | Yes |
| Persons involved in Real Estate Closings and Settlements | Currently exempt under 31 CFR § 103.170. | An ANPRM was issued at 68 FR 17569 (April 10, 2003). | No | No | No | Yes | No |
| Telegraph Companies | Currently exempt under 31 CFR § 103.170. | | No | No | No | Yes | No |
| Commodity Trading Advisors | Currently exempt under 31 CFR § 103.170. | Proposed AML Rule at 68 FR 23640 (May 5, 2003). | No | No | No | Yes | No |
| Investment Companies (other than mutual funds) | Currently exempt under 31 CFR § 103.170. | | No | No | No | Yes | No |

## Appendix B: Anti-Money Laundering Statistics[1]

| FBI Program | FY2002 | FY2003 | FY2004 | FY2005 |
|---|---|---|---|---|
| White Collar Crime | 507 | 402 | 500 | 418 |
| Organized Crime/ Drug | 315 | 347 | 261 | 160 |
| Criminal Enterprise[2] | 19 | 38 | 44 | 98 |
| Cyber Crime | 6 | 10 | 18 | 20 |
| Violent Crime | 7 | 12 | 4 | 5 |
| Other | 2 | 59 | 54 | 65 |
| TOTAL | 856 | 868 | 881 | 766 |

Table 1 FBI money laundering informations[3] and indictments, FY2002–FY2005

| | FY2002 | FY2003 | FY2004 | FY2005 |
|---|---|---|---|---|
| Arrests | 429 | 342 | 353 | 253 |
| Convictions | 731 | 512 | 459 | 440 |
| Restitution | $2.1b | $706m | $2.1b | $2.4b |
| Recoveries[4] | $18.1m | $15.6m | $1.9m | $10.2m |
| Fines | $11.3m | $108.1m | $29.4m | $15.8m |

Table 2 FBI money laundering-related statistics, FY2002 – FY2005

| | FY2003 | FY2004 | FY2005 |
|---|---|---|---|
| Investigations | 236 | 253 | 319 |
| Arrests | 76 | 112 | 156 |

Table 3  DEA Office of Financial Operations investigative statistics, FY 2003–FY2005

[1]  Law enforcement agencies working together on investigative task forces may report the same convictions, forfeitures, and other relevant money laundering statistics in individual agency data.

[2]  A "criminal enterprise" in this context refers to violent gangs and theft rings

[3]  A grand jury must approve an indictment, while a prosecutor can issue an "information" without grand jury approval.  Both accuse the defendant of committing a crime.

[4]  A "recovery" involves funds intercepted by the FBI before being accessed by a criminal enterprise.  A recovery may involve judicial proceedings.

| | FY2003 | FY2004 | FY2005 | FY2006 (as of 8/31/2006) |
|---|---|---|---|---|
| Investigations Initiated | 1590 | 1789 | 1639 | 1369 |
| Indictments/ Informations | 1041 | 1304 | 1147 | 962 |
| Sentenced | 667 | 687 | 782 | 738 |
| Forfeitures | 600 | 1593 | 1667 | |
| Forfeiture Amount | $73.3m | $59.7m | $123.3m | |

Table 4 IRS-CI Money Laundering Statistics, FY 2003-2006 (as of 8/31/06)

| | FY2003 | FY2004 | FY2005 |
|---|---|---|---|
| Arrests | 314 | 421 | 340 |
| Indictments | 360 | 499 | 378 |

Table 5  ICE prosecutions for money laundering offences (18 U.S.C. 1956 and 1957).[5]

| | FY2003 | FY2004 | FY2005 |
|---|---|---|---|
| Arrests | 87 | 58 | 32 |
| Indictments | 124 | 133 | 75 |
| Convictions | 125 | 142 | 101 |

Table 6 ICE prosecutions for bulk cash smuggling  (31 USC 5332).

| | FY2003 | FY2004 | FY2005 |
|---|---|---|---|
| Arrests | 48 | 31 | 42 |
| Indictments | 31 | 34 | 34 |
| Convictions | 18 | 28 | 24 |

Table 7 ICE prosecutions for operating an unlicensed Money Services Business (18 U.S.C. 1960)

---

[5] USC 1956 criminalizes the laundering of the proceeds of specified unlawful activity in certain specified situations and 18  USC 1957 criminalizes the spending of proceeds of crime without the additional requirement (as in section 1956) that this spending be accompanied by criminal intent.

| Defendants Sentenced In FY2003 With 18 U.S.C. 1956 On Any Count Of Conviction | | |
| --- | --- | --- |
| | Count | Col% |
| Bank Robbery | 1 | 0.1% |
| Drugs: Trafficking | 277 | 29.00% |
| Firearms: Use | 1 | 0.1% |
| Larceny | 3 | 0.3% |
| Fraud | 46 | 4.80% |
| Embezzlement | 1 | 0.10% |
| Money Laundering | 596 | 62.40% |
| Racketeering | 29 | 3.00% |
| Immigration | 1 | 0.10% |
| TOTAL | 955 | 100% |

Table prepared by the Department of Justice Office of Policy and Legislation, Criminal Division, from data provided by the U.S. Sentencing Commission

**Table 8  18 USC 1956 criminalizes the laundering of the proceeds of specified unlawful activity in certain specified situations.**

| Defendants Sentenced In FY2003 With 18 U.S.C. 1957 On Any Count Of Conviction | | |
| --- | --- | --- |
| | Count | Col% |
| Murder | 1 | 0.61% |
| Drugs: Trafficking | 16 | 9.82% |
| Larceny | 5 | 3.10% |
| Fraud | 37 | 22.70% |
| Embezzlement | 2 | 1.20% |
| Forgery/Counterfeiting | 1 | 0.61% |
| Money Laundering | 97 | 59.50% |
| Racketeering | 1 | 0.61% |
| Immigration | 1 | 0.61% |
| Administration of Justice Related | 1 | 0.61% |
| TOTAL | 163 | 100% |

Table prepared by the Department of Justice Office of Policy and Legislation, Criminal Division, from data provided by the U.S. Sentencing Commission

**Table 9  18 USC 1957 criminalizes the spending of proceeds of crime without the additional requirement (as in section 1956) that this spending be accompanied by criminal intent.**

| Defendants Sentenced In FY2003 With 18 U.S.C. 1960 On Any Count Of Conviction | | |
|---|---|---|
| | Count | Col% |
| Drugs: Trafficking | 1 | 5.60% |
| Money Laundering | 14 | 77.80% |
| Immigration | 1 | 5.60% |
| Administration of Justice Related | 1 | 5.60% |
| National Defense | 1 | 5.60% |
| TOTAL | 18 | 100.00% |

Table prepared by the Department of Justice Office of Policy and Legislation, Criminal Division, from data provided by the U.S. Sentencing Commission

**Table 10  18 USC 1960 criminalizes the operation of an unlicensed money transmitting business**

| Defendants Sentenced In FY2003 With 31 U.S.C. 5313 On Any Count Of Conviction | | |
|---|---|---|
| | Count | Col% |
| Money Laundering | 7 | 87.50% |
| Immigration | 1 | 12.50% |
| TOTAL | 8 | 100.00% |

Table prepared by the Department of Justice Office of Policy and Legislation, Criminal Division, from data provided by the U.S. Sentencing Commission

**Table 11  31 U.S.C. 5313 criminalizes the failure to file a report on domestic coin and currency transactions exceeding $10,000**

| Defendants Sentenced In FY2003 With 31 U.S.C. 5316 On Any Count Of Conviction | | |
|---|---|---|
| | Count | Col% |
| Drugs: Trafficking | 1 | 1.40% |
| Larceny | 1 | 1.40% |
| Fraud | 2 | 2.90% |
| Money Laundering | 64 | 91.40% |
| Immigration | 1 | 1.40% |
| Traffic Violations and Other | 1 | 1.40% |
| TOTAL | 70 | 100.00% |

Table prepared by the Department of Justice Office of Policy and Legislation, Criminal Division, from data provided by the U.S. Sentencing Commission

**Table 12  31 U.S.C. 5316 requires individuals to report the transport or transfer of more than $10,000 in currency or monetary instruments into or out of the United States  The form that must be filed is titled: Report of International Transportation of Currency or Monetary Instruments (CMIR).**

| Defendants Sentenced In FY2003 With 31 U.S.C. 5324 On Any Count Of Conviction | | |
| --- | --- | --- |
| | Count | Col% |
| Banks: Robbery | 1 | 1.20% |
| Drugs: Trafficking | 7 | 8.60% |
| Firearms: Use | 1 | 1.20% |
| Fraud | 12 | 14.80% |
| Tax Offenses | 2 | 2.50% |
| Money Laundering | 55 | 67.90% |
| Immigration | 1 | 1.20% |
| Traffic Violations and Other | 2 | 2.50% |
| TOTAL | 81 | 100.00% |

Table prepared by the Department of Justice Office of Policy and Legislation, Criminal Division, from data provided by the U.S. Sentencing Commission

**Table 13   31 U.S.C. 5324 makes it crime to structure transactions to avoid the reporting requirement on transport or transfer of more than $10,000 in currency or monetary instruments into or out of the U.S.**

| Defendants Sentenced In FY2003 With 31 U.S.C. 5332 On Any Count Of Conviction | | |
| --- | --- | --- |
| | Count | Col% |
| Larceny | 4 | 9.80% |
| Fraud | 6 | 14.60% |
| Money Laundering | 23 | 56.10% |
| Immigration | 2 | 4.90% |
| Offenses in Prison | 1 | 2.40% |
| Administration of Justice Related | 1 | 2.40% |
| Traffic Violations and Other | 4 | 9.80% |
| TOTAL | 41 | 100.00% |

Source:  Table prepared by the Department of Justice Office of Policy and Legislation, Criminal Division, from data provided by the U.S. Sentencing Commission

**Table 14   31 U.S.C. 5332 makes it a crime for anyone with the intent to evade the CMIR requirement to knowingly conceal more than $ 10,000 in currency or monetary instruments and to transport or transfer or attempt to transport or transfer such currency or monetary instruments into or out of the United States**

|                                          | FY2002 | FY2003 | FY2004 | FY2005 |
|------------------------------------------|--------|--------|--------|--------|
| Defendants convicted of 18 USC 1956      | 1,034  | 955    | 970    | 749    |
| Defendants convicted of 18 USC 1957      | 217    | 163    | 178    | 326    |
| TOTAL                                    | 1,251  | 1,118  | 1,148  | 1,075  |

Table 15   Source: Department of Justice Office of Policy and Legislation, Criminal Division

| Statute | Defendants | Cases | Defendants Convicted |
|---------|------------|-------|----------------------|
| 18 U.S.C. § 1956 | 2219 | 838 | 970 |
| 18 U.S.C. § 1957 | 455 | 291 | 178 |
| 18 U.S.C § 1960 | 68 | 45 | 27 |
| 18 U.S.C. § 982 | 705 | 253 | 163 |
| 31 U.S.C. § 5313 | 28 | 14 | 9 |
| 31 U.S.C. § 5316 | 109 | 99 | 67 |
| 31 U.S.C. § 5317 | 39 | 27 | 6 |
| 31 U.S.C. § 5324 | 219 | 145 | 95 |
| 31 U.S.C. § 5332 | 152 | 115 | 60 |
| TOTAL | 3994 | 1827 | 1575 |

Table 16  Money laundering-related prosecution statistics for FY2004.  Source: Department of Justice Office of Policy and Legislation, Criminal Division

| Federal Regulator | BSA/AML Exams conducted in FY 2005 | Formal Enforcement Actions[6] taken in FY 2005 |
|-------------------|-----------------------------------|-----------------------------------------------|
| Federal Deposit Insurance Corporation | 2,755 | 16 |
| Federal Reserve | 682 | 9 |
| National Credit Union Association | 4,715 | 0 |
| Office of the Comptroller of the Currency | 1,530 | 32 |
| Office of Thrift Supervision | 722 | 14 |
| Internal Revenue Service[7] | 5 | 0 |
| TOTAL | 10,409 | 71 |

Table 17  Depository financial institution Bank Secrecy Act (BSA) compliance examinations and formal enforcement actions taken in FY2005 by Federal banking regulators and the Internal Revenue Service, which has been delegated the authority to examine, for BSA compliance, all financial institutions not currently examined by a Federal functional regulator

---

[6]  A formal enforcement action is a supervisory action used to compel a bank to address serious violations of the law.  Examples of these types of actions are Orders to Cease and Desist and Civil Money Penalties.  Formal actions generally are public.  In addition, the regulators took in excess of 2,000 "informal" enforcement actions, which relate primarily to technical violations of the BSA requirements.

[7]  The IRS has been delegated the authority to examine for BSA compliance all financial institutions not currently examined by a Federal functional regulator. This includes the financial institutions listed in Table 18

| Examination Subject | FY 2005 | FY 2006 (through 7/29/06) |
| --- | --- | --- |
| Credit Union | 8 | 8 |
| Casino | 21 | 6 |
| Card Club | 13 | 9 |
| Check Casher | 1,485 | 1,970 |
| Currency Dealer | 26 | 29 |
| Issuer of Money Orders | 65 | 55 |
| Money Transmitter | 1,271 | 1,773 |
| Nevada Casino | 1 | 0 |
| Seller/Redeemer of Traveler's Checks | 752 | 1,016 |
| Seller/Redeemer of Stored Value Cards | 0 | 11 |
| Tribal Casinos/Card Clubs | 3 | 2 |
| Undesignated | 67 | 82 |
| TOTAL | 3,712 | 4,961 |

**Table 18  IRS SB/SE BSA Civil Examinations Completed**

## Appendix C: Law Enforcement Data and Intelligence Centers

| Name | Lead Agency | Participating Agencies | How It Works |
|---|---|---|---|
| Data Analysis and Research for Trade Transparency System (DARTTS) | ICE | Customs Services of Colombia, Paraguay, Brazil, and Argentina | DARTTS is an analytical data system that identifies anomalies in important and export data. It has the ability to track the movement of people, money, and cargo into and out of the United States. |
| Money Laundering Coordination Center (MLCC) | ICE | | MLCC is a depository for intelligence information gathered through undercover money laundering investigations and functions as the coordination center for both domestic and international undercover money laundering operations. MLCC also provides information to investigators about the movement of proceeds through the Black Market Peso Exchange. |
| Law Enforcement Support Center (LESC), Williston, VT | ICE | Federal, State, and local law enforcement community | Primary users of the LESC are law enforcement agencies that need information about foreign nationals they may encounter. They can contact the LESC through the International Justice and Public Safety Information Sharing Network or by calling an 800#. LESC receives over 60,000 queries monthly. ICE is exploring the creation of a bulk cash smuggling center within LESC to serve as a bulk currency smuggling information, deconfliction, and investigative support center. |
| Blue Lightning Operation Coordination Center (BLOCC)/ Gulf Coast HIDTA, Gulfport, MS | ICE | Federal, State and local law enforcement agencies in LA, AL, MS, GA, AR, NC, SC, TN, and part of Texas have access to TECS | Responds to queries 24/7 re: individuals/ vehicles/info through TECS; BLOCC sends out daily e-mail intelligence summary, plus bulletins. |
| Treasury Enforcement Communications System (TECS) | ICE | 34 Federal, State and local agencies have access to TECS databases | TECS is CBP's operations system and ICE's investigative database for case management. It contains data relating to domestic and international financial crimes, including bulk currency smuggling violations, CMIR violations, and money laundering cases. TECS holds data regarding over $2.5 billion in currency seizures, as well as phone numbers and financial records of suspects. Phone numbers are cross-referenced with DEA's Special Operations Division (see below). |

| Name | Lead Agency | Participating Agencies | How It Works |
|------|-------------|------------------------|--------------|
| Tampa Lead Development Center (LDC), Tampa, FL | IRS–CI | Selected points of contact at IRS–CI field offices and LDC personnel. | The bulk currency database located at Tampa LDC contains intelligence data from IRS-CI bulk currency field offices (Dallas, Chicago, Nashville, Charlotte, New Orleans, St. Louis, Houston, and San Antonio). The goal is to run intelligence queries against data contained in other IRS databases (wire remitter, counterterrorism, and tax information) for reactive and proactive case development |
| OCDETF Fusion Center (OFC), Vienna, VA | DEA/ IRS–CI | ATF, DEA, FBI, IRS–CI, United States Marshal Service, FinCEN, EPIC, NDIC, United States Coast Guard | OFC is an intelligence center that can draw from existing data of participating agencies. OFC collects, analyzes, and mines drug and related financial investigation information to support coordinated multi-jurisdictional investigations focused on drug trafficking and money laundering enterprises. (DEA Special Operations Division acts as central contact/deconfliction point for field offices to gather OFC data) |
| Special Operations Division (SOD), Chantilly, VA | DEA | DEA, FBI, ICE, IRS, USMS | SOD uses technology and the investigative and intelligence resources of participating agencies to target major drug trafficking organizations. SOD coordinates and supports multi-jurisdictional and multinational investigations. |
| El Paso Intelligence Center (EPIC), El Paso, TX | DEA | State, local, and Federal agencies. Coordinates with CBP, DEA, ICE, IRS–CI, Texas Dept. of Public Safety, COBIJA[1], HIDTAs, and FL Dept. of Law Enforcement | Operation Pipeline records seizures made from private cars and trucks; Operation Convoy records highway seizures involving commercial vehicles; and Operation Jetway records seizures from airports, train and bus stations, package shipment facilities, U.S. Post Offices, and airport hotels and motels. |

---

[1] Cobija (the Spanish word for "blanket") is a coordinated planning effort managed by the Arizona Partnership of the Southwest Border HIDTA to synchronize local, tribal, state, and Federal highway interdiction operations.

| Name | Lead Agency | Participating Agencies | How It Works |
|---|---|---|---|
| Post-Seizure Analysis Team (PSAT), Austin, TX | IRS-CI | IRS-CI, DEA, FBI, ICE, and Texas National Guard | PSAT obtains and analyzes real-time information from drug and currency seizures in the Gulf Coast corridor and Texas. PSAT maintains a database and provides investigative support such as the dissemination of intelligence, identification of criminal associates, linking of suspects to other investigations, and the creation of organizational charts/timelines/graphs of events and relationships. |
| U.S. Dept. of Transportation/ Federal Motor Carrier Safety Administration/ Drug Interdiction Assistance Program (DIAP) | DEA/ IRS-CI | DEA | DIAP provides training for State and local law enforcement involved in highway interdiction by commercial vehicles (trucks, tractor trailers, etc.). Hosts annual "Pipeline Conference". |
| Human Smuggling and Trafficking Center (HSTC), Washington, DC | ICE | ICE, Coast Guard, FBI, U.S. Attorney for Criminal Division, NCTC, CIA and NSA | HSTC is an interagency law enforcement, intelligence, and foreign policy fusion center and information clearinghouse. Focus is on human smuggling, trafficking, and criminal support of terrorist travel. Goal is to facilitate broad distribution of information, prepare strategic threat assessments, make recommendations for action, coordinate/ deconflict initiatives, and serve as point of contact for similar foreign centers/officials. |

## Appendix D:  The Strategic Use of Asset Forfeiture

A significant source of financial support for anti-money laundering task forces, training, and law enforcement innovation is the money seized and forfeited from criminal enterprises.  The Treasury and Justice Departments' Asset Forfeiture Funds serve a crucial role in the national strategy against money laundering.

United States Attorneys Offices use both criminal and civil asset forfeiture laws to strip away property derived from criminal activity such as narcotics violations, money laundering, racketeering and fraud, as well as property used to facilitate the commission of certain crimes.  Whether through civil or criminal proceedings, the laws governing asset forfeiture provide due process to all persons claiming an ownership interest in the property.

The United States Attorneys' work on judicial asset forfeitures resulted in an estimated recovery of $390,450,467 in forfeited cash and property during Fiscal Year 2004.  This represents an increase of 14 percent over Fiscal Year 2003.  Approximately $2,626,415, or less than 1 percent, of the forfeited property was retained for official law enforcement use.  Approximately $44,229,624 of asset forfeiture proceeds were applied to restitution in victim-related offenses

The United States Attorneys Offices filed asset forfeiture counts in 3,785 criminal cases, which sought forfeiture as a criminal penalty during Fiscal Year 2004, representing an increase of 9 percent over the prior year.  At the end of the fiscal year, there were 5,103 criminal asset forfeiture cases pending, an increase of 16 percent when compared to Fiscal Year 2003.  Additionally, 2,235 civil forfeiture actions were filed by the United States Attorneys during the fiscal year, an increase of 4 percent when compared

to the prior year.  The United States Attorneys also obtained 1,433 civil asset forfeiture judgments in favor of the United States during the year, which represents a 14 percent increase over the prior year.

The Federal law enforcement agencies that deposit forfeited assets into the Department of Justice forfeiture fund are the DEA, FBI, the former Immigration and Naturalization Service[1] , Food and Drug Administration, U.S. Marshals Service, and U.S. Postal Service (see Tables 18 and 19)

The Treasury Executive Office for Asset Forfeiture (TEOAF) administers the Treasury Forfeiture Fund, which is the receipt account for the deposit of non-tax forfeitures made by Treasury and Department of Homeland Security law enforcement agencies.  These include ICE, CBP, IRS-CI, U.S. Secret Service (USSS), and the former Bureau of Alcohol, Tobacco, and Firearms[2](see Table 20).  The forfeiture amounts deposited into the fund have grown steadily over the past 5 years.

TEOAF's strategy is to use asset forfeiture to dismantle large systemic criminal organizations.  TEOAF supports "high-impact" investigations, defined as cases with a forfeiture potential of greater than $100,000.  The percentage of the annual forfeiture amount that comes from these high-impact cases is TEOAF's key performance measure.  More than 75 percent of the forfeited assets that  come into the Treasury forfeiture fund each year come from high impact cases, although these cases account for only five to seven percent of all asset forfeiture cases (see Table 21).

---

[1]  ICE and CBP have absorbed the duties of the Immigration and Naturalization Service

[2]  The Homeland Security Act of 2002 split the former Bureau of Alcohol, Tobacco and Firearms (ATF) into two new organizations with separate functions. The Act created a new office within the Department of the Treasury, the Alcohol and Tobacco Tax and Trade Bureau, and shifted certain law enforcement functions of ATF to the Department of Justice.

TEOAF is using forfeited assets to fund innovative law enforcement programs that are not likely to be considered for appropriated funding until the "proof of concept" is established. Among such initiatives are investigative databases and data mining systems, forensic laboratories and other technology-related projects. Once the "proof of concept" is successfully established, these projects can be included in the agencies' base funding, which in turn frees resources to fund new initiatives seeking support from the Treasury Forfeiture Fund. The following are among the recent successful initiatives realized with the support of the Treasury Forfeiture Fund.

- ICE's Trade Transparency Units: By sharing and analyzing import and export data with foreign counterparts, ICE is able to identify discrepancies that can be indicative of trade-based money laundering (See Goal 4).

- IRS-CI's E-Crimes Technology and Support Center: Located in Springfield, VA, this lab provides 24-hour technical support to Computer Investigative Specialists in the field and maintains a state-of-the-art technical training facility. The Digital Data Input Center transcribes and stores records gathered in the investigative process, making retrieval and analysis more efficient for field agents.

- USSS Electronic Crimes Special Agent Program (ECSAP): This program provides basic and advanced computer training to USSS agents. ESCAP trains agents in: (1) basic electronic crime investigation techniques; (2) network intrusion investigations; and (3) computer forensics and digital evidence and investigations.

In addition to funding agency-specific initiatives, the Treasury Forfeiture Fund also supports broad-based training programs that address current issues in investigative techniques and asset forfeiture; identify and promote best practices; and foster cooperation among investigative agencies. TEOAF's training strategy mirrors its funding strategy, emphasizing innovative ideas and practices that lead to more effective prosecutions and forfeitures. Between 2003 and 2006, TEOAF developed six new training curricula and conducted 19 seminars attended by more than 2,200 agents from across the United States.

| DEPARTMENT OF JUSTICE ASSET SEIZURES AND FORFEITURES BY AGENCY FOR FISCAL YEAR 2004 | | | | | |
|---|---|---|---|---|---|
| AGENCY | FORFEITURE TYPE | SEIZED ASSETS | SEIZED VALUE | FORFEITED ASSETS | FORFEITED AMOUNT |
| Drug Enforcement Administration | Administrative | 11,639 | $260,669,786.50 | 10,699 | $216,235,774.96 |
| | Civil/Judicial | 2,001 | $122,250,783.24 | 1,147 | $79,957,319.37 |
| | Criminal | 1,590 | $76,602,535.23 | 1,146 | $ 66,485,824.53 |
| DEA TOTALS | | 15,230 | $459,523,104.97 | 12,992 | $362,678,918.86 |
| Federal Bureau of Investigation | Administrative | 1,387 | $62,803,379.11 | 1,104 | $55,834,952.99 |
| | Civil/Judicial | 774 | $102,658,679.48 | 579 | $86,484,310.09 |
| | Criminal | 1,686 | $113,793,994.87 | 1,190 | $55,561,737.25 |
| FBI TOTALS | | 3,847 | $279,256,053.46 | 2,873 | $197,881,000.33 |
| Food and Drug Administration | Civil/Judicial | 18 | $2,508,102.12 | 4 | $775,822.92 |
| | Criminal | 8 | $ ,556,739.00 | 2 | $1,255,000.00 |
| FDA TOTALS | | 26 | $4,064,841.12 | 6 | $2,030,822.92 |
| Department of Homeland Security | Administrative | 0 | $0 | 3,899 | $8,098,066.23 |
| | Civil/Judicial | 4 | $1,457,599.84 | 22 | $2,029,897.82 |
| | Criminal | 1 | $1 | 20 | $557,747.37 |
| DHS TOTALS | | 5 | $1,457,600.84 | 3,941 | $10,685,711.42 |
| U.S. Marshals Service | Civil/Judicial | 22 | $33,101,708.76 | 24 | $30,872,594.21 |
| | Criminal | 49 | $1,281,103.81 | 44 | $1,679,262.62 |
| USMS TOTALS | | 71 | $34,382,812.57 | 68 | $32,551,856.83 |
| U.S. Postal Service | Civil/Judicial | 117 | $6,261,092.81 | 77 | $3,654,475.65 |
| | Criminal | 218 | $19,622,549.82 | 166 | $4,927,405.58 |
| USPS TOTALS | | 335 | $25,883,642.63 | 243 | $8,581,881.23 |
| FY 2004 TOTALS | | 19,514 | $804,568,055.59 | 20,123 | $614,410,191.59 |

Table 19

## DEPARTMENT OF JUSTICE ASSET SEIZURES AND FORFEITURES BY AGENCY FOR FISCAL YEAR 2005

| AGENCY | FORFEITURE TYPE | SEIZED ASSETS | SEIZED VALUE | FORFEITED ASSETS | FORFEITED AMOUNT |
|---|---|---|---|---|---|
| Drug Enforcement Administration | Administrative | 10,903 | $321,358,941.29 | 10,957 | $295,265,225.97 |
| | Civil/Judicial | 2,106 | $119,286,467.87 | 1,214 | $51,911,270.68 |
| | Criminal | 1,380 | $107,318,909.36 | 1,122 | $49,196,100.56 |
| DEA TOTALS | | 14,389 | $547,964,318.52 | 13,293 | $396,372,597.21 |
| Federal Bureau of Investigation | Administrative | 1,504 | $52,050,695.67 | 1,191 | $46,372,723.73 |
| | Civil/Judicial | 824 | $266,200,272.30 | 594 | $197,789,177.76 |
| | Criminal | 1,715 | $310,745,786.13 | 1,289 | $93,402,716.81 |
| FBI TOTALS | | 4,043 | $628,996,754.10 | 3,074 | $337,564,618.30 |
| Food and Drug Administration | Civil/Judicial | 24 | $5,799,790.77 | 4 | $905,845.00 |
| | Criminal | 58 | $6,150,357.94 | 41 | $4,839,648.35 |
| FDA TOTALS | | 82 | $11,950,148.71 | 45 | $5,745,493.35 |
| Department of Homeland Security | Civil/Judicial | 20 | $1,832,018.10 | 24 | $2,770,588.33 |
| | Criminal | 0 | $0 | 6 | $92,819.96 |
| DHS TOTALS | | 20 | $1,832,018.10 | 30 | $2,863,408.29 |
| U.S. Marshals Service | Civil/Judicial | 24 | $10,321,100.47 | 29 | $8,082,023.08 |
| | Criminal | 33 | $1,513,288.99 | 52 | $349,444.15 |
| USMS TOTALS | | 57 | $11,834,389.46 | 81 | $8,431,467.23 |
| U.S. Postal Service | Civil/Judicial | 193 | $43,158,507.65 | 70 | $6,633,797.95 |
| | Criminal | 187 | $10,977,524.37 | 220 | $9,742,585.49 |
| USPS TOTALS | | 380 | $54,136,032.02 | 290 | $16,376,383.44 |
| FY 2005 TOTALS | | 18,971 | $1,256,713,660.91 | 16,813 | $767,353,967.82 |

Table 20

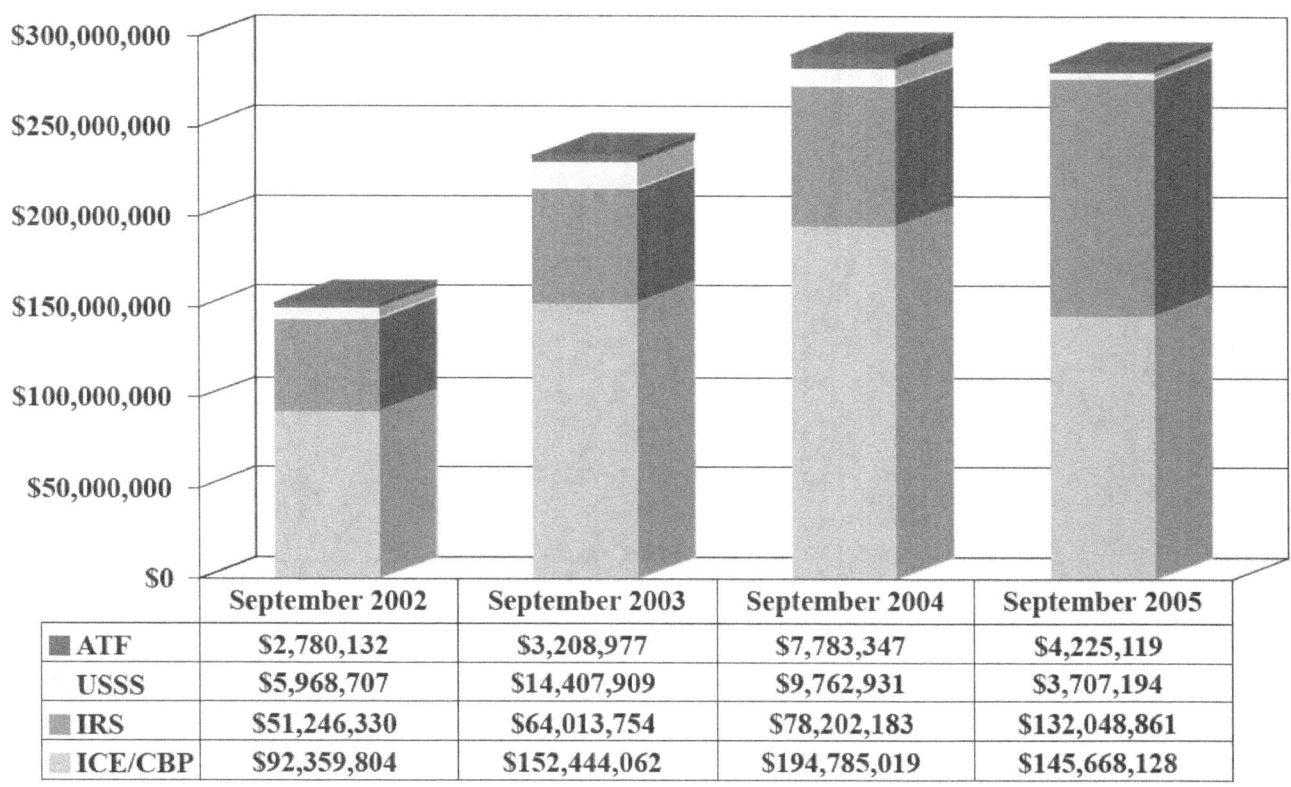

| | September 2002 | September 2003 | September 2004 | September 2005 |
|---|---|---|---|---|
| ATF | $2,780,132 | $3,208,977 | $7,783,347 | $4,225,119 |
| USSS | $5,968,707 | $14,407,909 | $9,762,931 | $3,707,194 |
| IRS | $51,246,330 | $64,013,754 | $78,202,183 | $132,048,861 |
| ICE/CBP | $92,359,804 | $152,444,062 | $194,785,019 | $145,668,128 |

Table 21 TEOAF deposits by agency at fiscal year end, 2002–2005[3].

| TEOAF High Impact Forfeiture Cases (currency forfeitures > $100,000 as a % of all forfeiture cases and of all forfeited assets) | | | | | | |
|---|---|---|---|---|---|---|
| | FY00 | FY01 | FY02 | FY03 | FY04 | FY05 |
| % Of All Forfeiture Cases | 5% | 7% | 5% | 6% | 6% | 7% |
| % Of All Forfeited Assets | 72% | 79% | 73% | 81% | 84% | 81% |

Table 22 TEOAF's emphasis on "high impact" cases is demonstrated in forfeiture statistics, FY2000–2005

---

[3] Prior to March 2003, the ICE/CBP seizures were accomplished by the legacy U.S. Customs Service.